Akikazu Hashimoto • Mike Mochizuki • Kurayoshi Takara

EDITORS

The Okinawa Question

and the U.S.-Japan Alliance

THE GEORGE WASHINGTON UNIVERSITY

THE ELLIOTT SCHOOL
OF INTERNATIONAL AFFAIRS

THE SIGUR CENTER FOR ASIAN STUDIES

Table of Contents

Military Transformation and Regional Security

Preface

After the September 11, 2001 terrorist attacks, the United States under the administration of President George W. Bush has been promoting a global reorganization of its military. In East Asia, this so-called military transformation started with changes in U.S. troop deployments in South Korea, but it has now begun to affect the American military presence in Japan.

To examine how the post-9/11 strategic environment affects the U.S.-Japan Security Alliance and Okinawa, eleven specialists from Japan and the United States initiated this project entitled "The Okinawa Question and the U.S.-Japan Alliance" in summer 2003. The Okinawa Question 2004 Japan-U.S. Action Committee, chaired by Akikazu Hashimoto and Kurayoshi Takara, was established to oversee this endeavor in Japan, and the Sigur Center for Asian Studies of the Elliott School of International Affairs at the George Washington University managed the project on the American side. By drawing upon the intellectual resources of Okinawa, Tokyo, and Washington, this project has sought to incorporate the Okinawan perspective in considering the proper form of the U.S.-Japan Security Alliance in the twenty-first century and the role of this alliance for Asia-Pacific security. While the Japanese and American members of this project see the need to reduce the burden of U.S. military bases and forces in Okinawa, we also recognize the positive contribution of the U.S.-Japan Security Alliance for regional and international security.

In October 2003, a workshop of all the project participants was held in Tokyo to discuss initial drafts of the chapters included in this report. In March 2004, a public conference was convened in Washington, D.C., to engage the U.S. policy community about strategic issues related to the alliance and Okinawa. At both meetings, a major concern was the delay in the return of the U.S. Marine Corps' Futenma Air Station as mandated in the 1996 SACO (Special Action Committee on Okinawa) Final Report (see Appendix). Given its location next to a crowded section of the city of Ginowan, the air station has posed a great danger to Okinawan citizens, thereby risking Japanese public support for hosting U.S. military bases.

On August 13, 2004, the kind of accident that everyone feared actually happened. A large CH-53D helicopter from Futenma Air Station crashed and burst into flames on the campus of Okinawa International University, which is adjacent to the base. This accident clearly proved the danger of Futenma Air Station and further damaged the Okinawan residents' feelings toward the American bases. If a student or resident had been killed, the resulting ill will toward the bases could not have been alleviated and the U.S.-Japan Security Alliance would have suffered irreparable damage. Instead of being relieved that such a tragedy did not occur, we have to regard this accident as a serious warning message to expedite the return of Futenma and the reduction of U.S. military bases and forces in Okinawa.

The delay in the construction of the replacement facility has not been the only problem. There has been much dissatisfaction in Japan with the way the U.S. military handled the August 2004 helicopter crash, causing a rapid increase in the public's calls for fundamental revision of the Status of Forces Agreement. In addition, Okinawans viewed the U.S. military's cordoning off a section of the university as a serious infringement on the rights of Okinawa International University.

For the safety of Okinawan residents, it is the duty of the Japanese government to try to eliminate the dangers involved with Futenma as soon as possible. The United States must also ensure the safe use of its bases and realize the problems involved to successfully carry out its military transformation. The American intention is to strengthen the functions of its bases in Japan, but unless there is a quick solution to the Futenma issue and a guarantee of safety for the Okinawan residents, the U.S. will not be able to smoothly implement this transformation. But as this report repeatedly emphasizes, in addressing the concerns and welfare of Okinawa, we must also consider the overall strategic interests and thinking of Japan and the United States and the vexing regional security issues regarding North Korea's nuclear weapons program and China-Taiwan relations

As this report goes to press, Japanese and American officials have been engaged in discussions to reduce the burden on Okinawa, to realign U.S. military forces in Japan, and to enhance further security cooperation between Japan and the United States. The February 19, 2005 joint statement of the U.S.-Japan Security Consultative Committee (the so-called "two-plus-two" committee of the U.S. secretaries of state and defense and the Japanese ministers of foreign affairs and defense) officially summarizes the bilateral dialogue thus far (see Appendix). Numerous media reports suggest that the U.S. and Japanese governments are also considering turning over the administration of several American military bases in Japan to the Japanese Self-Defense Forces and promoting joint Japan-U.S. use. Although such a shift will certainly reduce the amount of Japanese and Okinawan land that would be technically under U.S. military control, what must not be forgotten is the actual impact that these military bases have on the daily lives of local citizens.

Akikazu Hashimoto
Mike Mochizuki
Kurayoshi Takara

March 25, 2005

Forward: Reflections on Okinawa[1]

Ryutaro Hashimoto
Former Prime Minister of Japan

W hen Japan surrendered on August 15, 1945, I was in my second year of elementary school. It was only after the Battle of Okinawa began that I first heard the name "Okinawa." I had already learned about the "Nansei Islands" after my oldest cousin became lost at sea in that area while flying on a patrol. After American forces had landed on Okinawa, I was listening to the radio and heard about a place called "Okinawa." Having listened alongside me, my mother told me that Okinawa was part of the Nansei Islands, where my oldest cousin Genzaburo had died.

First Visit to Okinawa

My first trip to Okinawa occurred right after Prime Minister Eisaku Sato's visit to the island. In his capacity as President of the Liberal Democratic Party (LDP), the Prime Minister told some of us younger members of the party to go to Okinawa and speak with the local people. So, in August of that year, we formed a delegation and went. Looking back, there were three members including myself who would later become prime minister, Mr. Sosuke Uno, the delegation's leader, and Mr. Keizo Obuchi. For me, the images of Okinawa that I brought back from that trip still linger in my mind.

---

[1] These were remarks made by former Prime Minister Ryutaro Hashimoto at the Tokyo workshop of this project held on October 21, 2003.

There is a memorial park around Mabuni that is very beautiful now, but at the time of my visit, there were still unexploded bombs along the roadside. In addition, some local people could still be seen collecting bones of battle victims, which they put into a memorial tower. I was most surprised, however, by the fact that there were no trees taller than me. Those that had been taller were made shorter by bomb blasts.

After this tragic period of war, it took a very long time for Okinawa to adapt to the changes that occurred during the U.S. military occupation, Okinawa's return to Japan, and its incorporation into the Japanese system. The island also had issues and problems that the main Japanese islands did not, such as children of mixed ethnicity, children under six who were injured during the war, and other war-related issues, like the Tsushimamaru Case. During my trip, I handled and became quite familiar with these difficult issues in the Ministry of Health and Welfare, but I did not fully understand the problems that Okinawa faces as a result of the continued U.S. military presence.

The Rape

After this trip, I lost contact with Okinawa for a while, but then the LDP, the Socialist Party, and the Sakigake Party joined forces and the Murayama Cabinet was formed. I was appointed minister of the Ministry of International Trade and Industry (MITI), but the main issue at that time was not trade. The focus was the 1995 rape of a young girl by U.S. servicemen in Okinawa, which brought tension to the prefectural and national governments' relationships with the U.S. military.

While I was in London attending the 27th Trade Ministers' Quadriateral Meeting, there was a large protest by citizens in Okinawa. Without knowing much about the rape, I suddenly saw news about the protest on the BBC and something caught my attention. I turned to the other trade ministers from Canada, the European Union, the United Kingdom, and the United States, and told them, "Look how orderly this protest is. Even though harsh words are being tossed around, there are no placards that say, for example, 'America, go home!' or 'U.S. military, go home!'" The orderly nature of such a large-scale protest was surprising, especially to the Europeans who were used to such protests resulting in disorder.

Governor Ota and Futenma

When I replaced Prime Minister Murayama after he suddenly resigned, one of the major challenges that I took on was how to continue our relationship with the U.S. while trying to improve Tokyo's strained relationship with Okinawa Prefecture. I hoped to address this challenge at my first meeting with President Clinton in Santa Monica, California. Before doing so, however, I met with Okinawa Prefectural Governor Masahide Ota.

Though we had different positions and ideas, Governor Ota was very frank and honest with me. There were many problems between Okinawa and the Tokyo government at the time, but Governor Ota put all those aside and focused on the Futenma Air Station relocation issue. He emphasized that relocation is necessary to avoid accidents and other dangers. Since then I have gone to Futenma many times and have come to understand Governor Ota's words. However, no one in the Japanese government supported me in adding the Futenma issue to the agenda of my first meeting with President Clinton.

So, without a clear strategy, I made the trip to Santa Monica. During my conversation with President Clinton, he asked me, "Is there anything else you want to say?" After pointing out that I was not speaking on behalf of the Japanese government, I took this opportunity to tell him about my talk with Governor Ota and how he had emphasized the Futenma relocation issue. I also told him how all members of the Japanese government were opposed to my even broaching this subject with him. I continued by saying that I know this is not an easy problem to solve, but for the sake of the Okinawan people, it would be great if Japan and the U.S. could at least discuss what kinds of solutions are possible.

President Clinton listened carefully to my words and I still remember thinking that I could talk about anything with this person. I felt that with President Clinton, we could reexamine all aspects of the U.S.-Japan Security Alliance. Maybe we could even tackle other issues that have long been left unresolved.

U.S.-Japan Joint Declaration on Security

In April 1996, President Clinton and I signed the Joint Declaration on Security during his official visit to Japan. From there, the Japanese government started examining what new domestic laws would need to be written, what current laws could be used, and if an emergency measures law had to be established. We were not able to finish this work while I was prime minister, but if we had not started the process, then it would have been difficult to create the Anti-Terrorism Special Measures Law in Japan after September 11, 2001.

As a politician, I feel that signing this joint declaration with President Clinton was my contribution to my country and to U.S.-Japan relations. Of course, I was lucky to have Clinton by my side as well as U.S. Ambassador to Japan Walter Mondale and U.S. Secretary of Defense William Perry. I want to emphasize that though I went to the Santa Monica meeting without the support of my government on the Futenma relocation issue, Ambassador Mondale and Secretary Perry really helped me push this issue forward.

Since then, the importance of the Okinawa issue in international affairs has increased even more. Though there is much debate in Okinawa about the Special Action Committee on Okinawa (SACO) Final Report (See Appendix), for example, the fact that there is an effort to move Futenma to an offshore area shows that there is still trust that remains between the U.S. and Japan.

Last fall I had a chance to see President Clinton when he was in Tokyo during a lecture tour. We reminisced on old times over drinks, and he still remembered the Futenma issue. He mentioned that at the Kyushu-Okinawa Summit 2000, after I had resigned as prime minister, he saw the bases and told the Okinawan people that he recognized their hardships. He said that, for the sake of international relations, this issue needs to be resolved and told me how glad he was that we issued our joint statement on the U.S.-Japan Security Treaty when we did.

Okinawa's Strategic Importance

Looking at the records from World War II, until the end of the war, Japan's leaders did not know whether the decisive battle would be in Okinawa or Taiwan. In other words, Japan did not have a good sense of Okinawa's strategic importance.

During an exchange between President Franklin Roosevelt and Generalissimo Chiang Kai-shek, there was a proposal that the Republic of China (R.O.C.) occupy Okinawa. Chiang Kai-shek declined the offer, saying it would be possible if both the R.O.C. and the U.S. were involved, but would be too much for the R.O.C. alone. Therefore, the R.O.C. also did not regard Okinawa's strategic value that highly.

Even the U.S. may not have known the extent of Okinawa's importance early on. After World War II began on December 8, 1941, the U.S. State Department developed in the spring of 1942 a plan to occupy Japan. The plan called for two different administrations: one for the main Japanese islands, down to Kyushu; and a separate one for the Nansei Islands, with Okinawa included.

When Japan surrendered on August 15, 1945, the U.S. did not know what to do with Okinawa. There was talk of whether General Douglas MacArthur, head of the allied occupation, would handle it, but in the end, Okinawa did not fall under his control. One big reason for this involves the Soviet Union's intention to take Japan's northern islands and even Hokkaido. The U.S. was willing to give the Soviets a limited voice in the MacArthur-directed *allied* occupation of the main Japanese islands, but it decided in 1946 not to allow any Soviet influence in Okinawa by removing the island from occupation control and leaving it under sole American administration.

In truth, in Okinawa's long and varied history, the U.S. has had the most understanding of the island's strategic importance, especially following the war. Japanese people, myself included, did not understand this importance, nor the weight of the burden we main islanders had placed on the Okinawan people.

Okinawa in Elections

During my term as prime minister, I campaigned around the country for an election for Japan's House of Councillors and often mentioned Okinawa. I did not receive much response from the Japanese people, however, and I remember finishing the election with a sense of regret. In the upcoming election for Japan's House of Representatives [held in November 2003], the media is not focusing on diplomatic or security issues. If these topics do come up, then the story usually relates to sending the Japanese Self-Defense Forces to Iraq. Even in the manifestos of the LDP and the Democratic Party of Japan, there is no serious discussion of Okinawa and its role in the U.S.-Japan Security Alliance. In this post 9/11 environment, we must put more effort toward security and stability for the sake of Japan and the rest of the world.

I really hope that this project leads to good conclusions and advice for the Japanese and American governments. The Japanese government is limited in what it can provide Okinawa right now, but it is making requests to the U.S. government in hopes of soon providing more. Even if only one or two of our requests are met, we can still help reduce the burden on Okinawa.

Strategic Visions: Perspectives from Okinawa, Japan, and the United States

The Aspirations of Okinawa

Kurayoshi Takara
University of the Ryukyus

T he "Okinawa Question" is a question of Japan's identity as a nation. Japan's current challenge is how to define its national interest in a manner that has the backing of the majority of Japanese people and that can support their long-term vision. In addressing this challenge, Japan cannot escape the "Okinawa Question." The unfocused nature of the debate has, however, caused the "Okinawa Question" to be continuously treated ambiguously in contemporary Japanese politics.

The main point of the "Okinawa Question" is that Okinawa is part of Japan. The formulation of the Japanese nation is not yet complete. It has developed as a nation from the past to the present, and will continue to do so into the future. We must recognize that the unique territory of Okinawa exists within this changing Japanese nation.

Okinawa as a Part of Japan

Reviewing history, Okinawa was known as the Ryukyu Islands until just over 120 years ago and clearly did not belong to the Japanese state system. The Kingdom of Ryukyu (1429-1879) endured in these islands for nearly five hundred years, prevailing as a nation completely separate from the Japanese state. In spring 1879, however, the nascent modern Japanese state appropriated the Kingdom of Ryukyu's sovereignty and took coercive measures to incorporate its territory and citizens. Okinawa has, as a result, a past that reflects a dramatic change from being independent islands to being part of Japanese territory.

Two important moments in history are the Battle of Okinawa (1945) at the end of World War II and the period of post-war American rule (1945-1972). The fierce land battle staged by both the U.S. and Japanese forces in Okinawa resulted in not only war casualties of approximately twenty-five percent of the local residents, but also the loss of nearly all the precious cultural heritage sites in the Kingdom of Ryukyu. Following defeat, Japan gave up authority over Okinawa and the U.S. administration converted Okinawa into a strategic military base. Thus, Okinawa experienced not only destruction by the war some sixty years ago, but also abandonment by its own government after the war and a major transfiguration into an island of military bases under American rule.

Nonetheless, following the post-war period, the Okinawan residents chose reversion to Japan instead of continuance of American rule or political independence. The people regarded Japan as a "fatherland" for Okinawa and overwhelmingly supported Okinawa's official reversion on May 15, 1972.

Now that over thirty years have passed, the overwhelming majority of Okinawans feel that Okinawa is a part of Japan and do not advocate secession or independence. In fact, Okinawa is completely devoid of political parties or associations that pursue such separatist objectives or have them as part of their platforms.

This illustrates at least two issues. One is that the various problems in Okinawa are part of Japan's national affairs and the Japanese government is therefore obligated to try and solve these problems. The other issue is that, assuming Okinawa will remain a part of Japan, the Okinawan residents should take part in shaping Japan both now and in the future. It is possible to discuss whether or not Okinawa should continue to remain part of Japan in the fields of thought or culture, but in terms of political reality the matter has already been resolved and Okinawa's responsibility to shape Japan should be examined on that basis.

Okinawa's Distrust of the National Government

There is, however, a serious matter that must not be overlooked. This involves a scenario in which Okinawans do not accept that they are part of Japan.

As is clear on a review of history, Okinawa has gone through a number of phases in becoming a part of Japanese society and has also chosen to belong to Japan in a political sense. This kind of historical experience, not seen in other regions of Japan, planted an "attitude of relativity" in Okinawan residents, an attitude which does not regard the Japanese nation as being self-evident. The concept of Japan conceived by these residents is persistently "Okinawa plus the main Japanese islands." It is by no means composed of Okinawa firmly attached to a well-defined Japan. Therefore, while there is agreement that Okinawa belongs to Japan as a system, Okinawans continue to question Japan as a nation.

The U.S. military base issue brings this aspect to the surface. This issue is causing political and factional friction among Okinawan residents over their assessment of the U.S.-Japan Security Alliance. Opponents of the alliance do not accept the bases in Okinawa, which the Japanese government is obligated to provide through the alliance. On the other hand, supporters of the alliance value the significance of the bases, but also strive for a reduction in the burden borne by the locality. This Okinawan political conflict, where the former group is known as reformist and the latter as conservative, still continues and is expected to continue for some time.

Nevertheless, it is important to point out that many Okinawan people hold a deep suspicion of the national government, which engenders the reformist-conservative political friction described above. Why is approximately seventy-five percent of the total land used exclusively by the U.S. military in Japan concentrated in the small prefecture of Okinawa? Why are Okinawan residents exposed to the lion's share of the alliance's harmful effects — including noise pollution, crimes, and accidents — when other Japanese pay little for the security it provides? Is it that being Okinawan means these unjust conditions must be borne? What is more, the U.S. bases were not built after 1972 when the Constitution of Japan was applied to Okinawa, they appeared before that, during the period of American rule that resulted from Japan's defeat in the war. This is why Okinawans think of the base issue in terms of their experiences during the Battle of Okinawa and their memories of the American occupation.

In this way, there is skepticism and dissatisfaction with the national government that is not normally seen in the reformist-conservative friction. This kind of situation gives rise to frequent feelings of "We in Okinawa alone suffer discriminatory treatment" and has further complicated the Okinawan base issue. The Japanese government has also not yet fully explained why the bases are necessary for the U.S.-Japan Security Alliance and what significance they hold for Japan's national interest. This has led to a critical and skeptical view of the government taking deep root among Okinawans, who wonder what kind of national interest is being pursued at the "sacrifice of Okinawa."

◼︎

The Distinction between the Principled View and the Operational View

Having confirmed that Okinawa reverted to Japan and that Okinawans have continuously questioned the behavior of the Japanese nation, how then should recognition of these two facts be used to resolve the Okinawan base issue?

The basic principle that should be examined is whether the U.S.-Japan Security Alliance is necessary for Asia-Pacific security. If deemed unnecessary, then an alternative security arrangement should be offered and explained to the Japanese and Okinawan people. Since the alliance will remain necessary for the near future, I will instead assess the effectiveness of the alliance and acknowledge the significance of Okinawa's U.S. bases.

When this issue is discussed, it is necessary initially to set aside the following factors: the historical problems concerning the circumstances under which the bases were constructed during the period of American rule, the "discriminatory condition" of seventy-five percent of the land for U.S. bases in Japan being unevenly distributed in Okinawa, and the accidents, crimes, and noise pollution caused by the bases.

The first issue that must be considered relates to the basic principles of Japan's security policy. We must examine why Okinawa's U.S. bases exist and how we should assess the U.S.-Japan Security Alliance. Problems including the history of the bases' creation, their uneven distribution, and the harm they cause are related to the implementation of the alliance and should be discussed *after* having clarified basic principles related to security policy. When this is done, then for the first time we can discuss whether improvements in base operations are necessary, or whether the U.S.-Japan Security Alliance itself needs to be changed. Opponents of the alliance believe that the various operational problems arise only because bases exist in the first place, and argue that the only solution is to dissolve the alliance and dismantle the Okinawan bases. Those who preach this doctrine must explain, however, how it is possible to plan our nation's security policy without the alliance and the bases.

The U.S.-Japan Security Alliance is effective in promoting Asia-Pacific security and it is difficult to conceive of that role becoming unnecessary in the near future. Furthermore, the security policy of our nation values the U.S.-Japan relationship. This policy is supported by the majority of the people, who expressed this support through elections, and as a voter residing in Okinawa, I would like to respect these feelings of the people. In this light, Okinawa's U.S. bases are

U.S. Secretary of Defense Donald Rumsfeld meets with Okinawa Governor Keiichi Inamine on November 16, 2003, in the city of Naha, Okinawa. (Okinawa Prefectural Government, Public Relations Division)

playing an important role for the alliance, and thus Okinawa is fulfilling its responsibility to take part in Japan's contribution to the alliance.

Economic issues and the relocation of the U.S. Marine Corps' Futenma Air Station became contested topics in the 1998 Okinawa gubernatorial election. Governor Masahide Ota, the incumbent, argued for the relocation of Futenma outside the prefecture or outside Japan, whereas the challenger Keiichi Inamine argued for relocation within the prefecture and subsequently won the election by an overwhelming margin. At the root of their arguments lay a difference in assessments of the U.S.-Japan Security Alliance and the Okinawa bases. Ota, who took a skeptical, negative view of the alliance, argued not only that Futenma should be relocated outside the prefecture or outside Japan, but also that all of Okinawa's U.S. bases should be dismantled in stages by 2015. In contrast, Inamine valued the alliance and accepted the significance of the bases, which made possible the decision to relocate Futenma within the prefecture. As expected, the issue of relocating Futenma was also contested in the 2002 Okinawa gubernatorial election and Governor Inamine, who again argued for relocation within the prefecture, soundly defeated the other candidates. In addition, Tateo Kishimoto, who shares Governor Inamine's key political views, has twice been successful in mayoral elections for the city of Nago.

So, what did these elections indicate about the will of the majority? They suggested that the majority favor a complete dismantlement of Futenma Air Station, because it is located in a densely populated area.

This action would eliminate the political and factional friction among Okinawans. However, doing so could negatively affect the operational capabilities of the U.S.-Japan Security Alliance. If an alternative facility for Futenma is necessary, the only choice is to move its functions, either within or outside Okinawa. If relocation outside Okinawa is not possible, the decision must be made to relocate within Okinawa, while preparing for the resulting Okinawan opposition. Though a difficult choice, just such a decision was made because there was a realization, for the time being, of the significance of the alliance and the Okinawan bases. In other words, Okinawa resolved to fulfill its responsibility to take part in Japan's contribution to the alliance.

Okinawa's Responsibility to Participate

Okinawa's continued participation in the alliance will come at a high price. While return of the dangerous Futenma Air Station is a welcome change, the price of that return will be a new base off the coast of the district of Henoko in Nago. Since seventy-five percent of the land for U.S. bases in Japan is concentrated in Okinawa and consequently the residents are harmfully affected, new burdens caused by bases should be avoided as much as possible. Despite this awareness, relocation to Nago was chosen because of Okinawa's acceptance of the alliance's importance.

Thanks to this acceptance, Okinawa has been able to promote its own interests and seek improvements in how the alliance and the bases are operated. Okinawa is fulfilling its responsibility to share the burden of the alliance, and therefore has ample right to discuss the circumstances in which it is placed.

The concentration in Okinawa of seventy-five percent of the land for bases is unfair, and progress is required in base reduction and consolidation in accordance with the Special Action Committee on Okinawa (SACO) Final Report (See Appendix) and in a way that is acceptable to the Okinawan people, who bear the burden of the bases. Discussion about our nation's security policy and the future of the U.S.-Japan Security Alliance should help in defining a level of reduction and consolidation acceptable to Okinawans. Since the U.S. government operates the Okinawan bases, it has an obligation to eliminate the various dangers, harmful effects, and crimes that emanate from the bases and should make earnest efforts to reduce Okinawa's burden and the risks involved.

Regardless of whether the problems of the U.S.-Japan Status of Forces Agreement can be resolved solely by reconsidering operations or whether drastic reform is necessary, improvements need to be made to the satisfaction of Okinawans. Their demands are not in conflict with the principle of valuing the U.S.-Japan Security Alliance. The people only seek improvements in the operation of the alliance and the bases, and both the U.S. and Japanese governments have a duty to respond in earnest to those demands.

There is a proposal for making the alternative facility for Futenma not solely for U.S. military use but also accessible by the private sector for joint military and civilian use. Another proposal calls for Futenma to be secured for use as part of Okinawa's infrastructure following its dismantling or relocation. In addition, there is a bold argument that the usage period for the alternative facility should be limited to fifteen years. Such proposals are concrete assertions and examples of how the Okinawans are seeking operational improvements.

The gist of the proposal to limit the usage period to fifteen years can be roughly summarized in three points. First, prior to use, it is necessary to guarantee a level of base operations that is acceptable to Okinawans. Secondly, after a fixed period following the start of use, Okinawa should assess whether the new base operations are still acceptable to its residents. The third point concerns a desire that, in the shortest time possible after the start of use, Asia-Pacific regional peace and stability will reach a point where the new base is no longer necessary. The figure of fifteen years encompasses these three points and represents Okinawa's wish to be an involved party in discussions concerning the operation of the alliance and the bases.

Regarding this desire of the Okinawan people, the Japanese prime minister, who holds power regarding the operation of the U.S.-Japan Security Alliance, should express that, "as the person responsible for Japan's affairs, I promise, with the understanding of the Okinawan residents, to create a level of security in the Asia-Pacific region as soon as possible so that the alternative facility for Futenma will become unnecessary."

Japan's Identity and Okinawa

Thus far, Okinawans have valued the U.S.-Japan Security Alliance and have accepted the U.S. bases, while expressing their wish to reduce the excessive risks and burden of the bases. Nonetheless, the residents are still filled with fundamental doubts, including the deep suspicion that Okinawa is appreciated only for its bases. Most residents would prefer that Okinawa use its historical and cultural achievements and geographical position to fulfill an independent role in the Asia-Pacific region, not a role for the U.S. military.

We should not remain content with the current security system which depends on Japan's relationship with the U.S. In the future, Japan should construct peaceful multilateral relationships which include the U.S., but also extend to nations such as China and the Koreas. As a result, a regional order or "East Asian Community" would emerge. If such an era is born, Okinawa should pay more attention to situations in the surrounding region, including the Taiwan-China issue and the Cheju Island-Korean Peninsula issue. It should support the stability of the "East Asian Community" and encourage cooperation among the surrounding nations. Alternatively, Okinawa should look beyond the Asia-Pacific region and show that it is a player not only in the military and security realm, but also in the intellectual realm.

Nonetheless, these 120 years or more of history, including the twenty-seven years of American rule, have limited Okinawa's options. At one time, Okinawa was just a group of poor outlying islands in the southern part of Japan. At another time, it was a group of islands with the purpose of preventing the U.S. from landing on the main Japanese islands. In the next period, it was a group of islands cut away from Japan and handed over to the American military. It is currently a group of islands that serves an indispensable military function for the U.S.-Japan Security Alliance, again a role and character not desired by the Okinawan residents.

What is being tested is actually Japan's national image, its identity. The main issue behind the "Okinawa Question" is about what kind of nation Japan wishes to become and what kind of security system it wishes to construct.

The significance of the current U.S.-Japan Security Alliance and the Okinawan bases should be defined by images of the future, such as how Japan's future identity should be created and how a security system that will form an important link with that identity should be constructed. Until Okinawa's base issue is regarded as being connected to these images, the debate over the issue will not be taken as seriously as is necessary.

Believing that Japan's future national image and identity will be discussed seriously, the majority of Okinawan residents are currently trying to fulfill their responsibility to participate in the alliance. They believe that doing so is necessary to keep their right to shape the Japanese nation. Thus is Okinawa's destiny.

Japan's National Identity and Asia-Pacific Security:
The Relevance of the Okinawa Perspective

Akikazu Hashimoto

National Graduate Institute for Policy Studies (Tokyo)

 he Japanese government has sent its first contingent of Self-Defense Forces abroad to participate in the occupation of Iraq. This historic juncture presents an opportune time for Japanese and American researchers to gather together and exchange candid opinions on Asia-Pacific security and to make specific policy recommendations to the governments of the United States and Japan.

The international climate currently surrounding our global society has undergone significant changes. Since the end of the Cold War in 1989, we have been beset by a string of events: the Persian Gulf War of 1991; the terrorist attacks on the U.S. on September 11, 2001; the war in Afghanistan; the war in Iraq of 2003; and the North Korea problem.

Domestic realities in Japan have also been radically altered. With the halt of its rapid economic growth at the end of 1991, Japan now needs to transform into a stable and mature society. The economy has been mired in a deflationary cycle and the political scene has been marked by dysfunction and plagued by a siege mentality since the end of the so-called 1955 System of one-party governments led by the Liberal Democratic Party. While society is quite optimistic in one sense, an increasing number of people also harbor uncertainties and fears.

Reconstruction of Japan's National Identity

In times like these, we should break away from a climate of policy postponement characterized by wasteful ad hoc policies and an avoidance of matters that need to be addressed. Now is the time to reaffirm what constitutes Japan's "identity," to reconstruct it, and to consider how Japan should formulate its foreign policy.

The desirable "identity" for Japan in terms of diplomacy should incorporate three elements:

- "Coexistence" based on a redefined relationship between "self" and "other" based on mutual respect and understanding.

- The Japanese spirit of polytheism that acknowledges and allows other gods.

- A more flexible perspective regarding the universalism of liberal democratic values.

We need to integrate these three elements into a new Japanese identity as a nation. By doing so, Japan will be better able to contribute to the international community of the twenty-first century. Based on this moral foundation, Japan can help resolve regional conflicts involving different cultures and civilizations and eradicate terrorism.

The first element involves countries and ethnic groups recognizing the notion of "others" (other countries) and "self" (own country), and how they form these "self-other" relationships with each other. Regardless of the nature of the relationship, it can never be an excuse for terrorism. But, any conflict or dispute between two nations that has arisen from a "self-other" relationship is particularly difficult to resolve peacefully. This is because neither party will back down from the legitimacy of their own argument. The U.S.-North Korea stand-off is a case in point. Peaceful conflict resolution first requires coexistence based on mutual respect.

Regarding the second element, compromise and reconciliation between the Christian religions (particularly the Protestants) and the Islamic faith will be difficult to achieve as long as both groups continue to maintain that their "God" is the one "true" god. This tendency is particularly strong among fundamentalists of these monotheistic faiths. This is not to say that their respective founders, Jesus Christ and Mohammed, were exclusionary. In fact, we should recall Christian and Islamic teachings that "all things on heaven and earth exist within God" (God embraces all things). Such teachings have elements that also resonate in Japanese Buddhism.

Concerning the third element, the value of liberal democracy certainly represents the most legitimate and desirable political mechanism for deciding and pursuing collective goals of a nation. But the concrete form and substance of this liberal democracy will inevitably be shaped by a nation's particular history and culture. Therefore, American attempts to promote its own style of democracy in other countries as a universal principle will naturally provoke opposition from other cultures and civilizations.

◼ ═══════════════════════════════════════

Pan-Asian Coexistence and the U.S.-Japan Security Alliance

The main aim of Japan after World War II was economic growth and the pursuit of ever-increasing wealth. This progressive view of history is crumbling, and one-country pacifism — where one tried to live in peace within one's own borders while shirking responsibilities to contribute to international security — is no longer acceptable in the international community. When looking at Japan from the perspective of other countries, the question arises as to what the present "Japan" actually represents.

Over the past few years, the world's, and in particular Asia's, view of Japan has become more critical. During his visit to Japan in June 2003, South Korean President Roh Moo-hyun noted in his speech to Japan's National Diet, "Every time there is an action by Japan that recalls our unfortunate shared history, the response of the people of Asia, including South Korea, shows their continued sensitivity. They are following the debates in Japan on defense and security arrangements and revision of the peace constitution with a mixture of suspicion and uncertainty." The president also regarded with "suspicion and uncertainty" the three National Emergency bills that passed on the day he arrived in Japan.

Since the terrorist attacks in the U.S. on September 11, 2001, there has been a strong sense that Japan's foreign policy, especially its security policy, has become totally preoccupied with ad hoc measures that only address the "symptoms" of various problems. Even in the aftermath of the war in Iraq of 2003, Japanese diplomacy has not yet established an identity and ad hoc measures continue. Spurred on by the fact that Japan's economy has not yet recovered, the question is what will happen to Asia's view of Japan? If Japan is regarded with suspicion and uncertainty, we cannot easily counter such sentiment.

Therefore, Japan needs to promote pan-Asian coexistence at the same time it strengthens its alliance with the United States. How then should Japan bring to life in its relations with countries of the Asia-Pacific region the three elements of a new national identity that I referred to earlier? First, Japan should promote in political terms an inclusive Asia-Pacific community that encompasses both the United States and China and should initiate regional discussions about collective security. Economically, Japan should facilitate mutual growth and prosperity by encouraging the development of a common regional currency by first calling for a regional basket of national currencies. Achieving these ambitious goals will require overcoming national differences through a polytheistic spirit and establishing the vitality of the people as the common foundation for international cooperation. In so doing, the peoples of Asia will be able to address the issue of how liberal democracy can incorporate the diversity of national characters and cultures.

Okinawa's Perspective

Why look at Japan from the perspective of Okinawa? One reason relates to the excessive burden of having seventy-five percent of the land for U.S. military bases in Japan located in Okinawa, which accounts for less than one percent of Japan's landmass, and the inconvenience, inequity, and injustice that this burden causes. Okinawan citizens have the right and the Japanese government the responsibility to reduce this burden. To do so, U.S. bases should be decreased, and the safety and peace of mind of Okinawans must be protected more effectively.

According to Derek J. Mitchell, Senior Fellow at Washington, D.C.'s Center for Strategic and International Studies, if the U.S. has long-range military capabilities that are quickly deployable and backed by technology, then it only needs to secure arrangements for sending troops to operational bases (hubs) within combat theaters as required, and not place so much emphasis on forward deployment to remote bases. He also notes that in an era of proliferation of short-range missiles, forward deployment bases are perceived to constitute an unnecessary weakness.

The U.S. Defense Department's *Quadrennial Defense Review Report* of 2001 emphasizes lightweight, highly mobile and flexible land forces capable of rapid deployment and movement; long-range, precise attack capabilities in a theater of war; and intelligence superiority and its integration through deployment of state-of-the-art command systems. In short, the new style of war will involve readily deployable, long-range military capabilities.

The Bush administration is seeking to reconstruct and reorganize its military capabilities in East Asia based on a review of military deployments on a global scale. Naturally, a review of military deploy–ments in Okinawa also falls within this scope and will have implications for the relocation of the U.S. Marine Corps' Futenma Air Station.

The Japanese government has decided to relocate Futenma to a facility offshore from the district of Henoko in the city of Nago and is now conducting an environmental impact assessment. When Governor Keiichi Inamine ran for a second term in office, he made a "fifteen-year" time limit *(kigen)* for the new Henoko offshore facility a major personal campaign pledge. The reasons behind such a pledge were not ill-founded, but the significant changes in U.S. global strategy and military tactics since 9/11 demand a more flexible approach. Members of both the Japanese and American governments, including military experts, often state, "Should there be a crisis in North Korea, deciding the time limit now is a naïve notion tantamount to sending aid to the enemy." But as Professor Takara has noted in Chapter I, such a quick dismissal of the "time limit" notion indicates insensitivity to the Okinawan desire to participate in meaningful discussions about the existence and operations of U.S. bases in Okinawa. We have to take a more flexible approach.

We need to bilaterally reexamine the intended use and "term" *(kikan)* once construction of the Henoko facility begins. Why use the word "term" *(kikan)* instead of "time-limit" *(kigen)*? An ending is implicit in the word "time-limit" but "term" allows for a renewal of the period based on a proper assessment of the situation in Asia at the time. Regardless of the changes that occur during the return, consolidation, and reduction of U.S. military bases, quick emergency response arrangements must remain in place to enable the U.S. to use the bases exclusively in an emergency.

The Japanese government, which bears responsibility for its land and its people, must acknowledge that the nation of Japan includes Okinawa. Therefore, it must reduce the dangers to Okinawa. An analogy can be drawn here between the pent-up frustrations of the people of Okinawa and a rumbling volcano. One can never know when either might erupt. As Governor Inamine stated in March 2001, "An incident in Okinawa [caused by the U.S. military] is not an isolated event, or a dot, but part of a continuous line laid down over fifty-six years. Within the broader context of history, who knows what will burst forth if that line is breached?"

A second reason why Japan should be viewed from the Okinawa perspective is because Okinawa reveals more about the future potential of both Japan and Asia in the twenty-first century than the Tokyo perspective. Of all of the places in Japan, Okinawa is located in closest proximity with much of East Asia. When one considers the future of Asian development and Japan's role in it, there is really no need to go all the way to Tokyo—Okinawa is a much closer gateway for connecting Asia and Japan. Moreover, because Okinawa has historically had deep interactions with the southern regions of China and Taiwan, it might be able to play a mediating role between the main islands of Japan and China.

But the significance of Okinawa for Japan goes well beyond matters of geography and history. In post-industrial society, the value of knowledge and information in both politics and economics has increased dramatically. As a consequence, people are searching for a new value system that might replace the old value system of industrial society. In this new value system, what will be emphasized is the ability to adapt to new social changes without being preoccupied with physical distances. We must be aware that existing societal structures will become even more stretched and reshaped because of the decline in the Japanese population, the aging of its people, and trends that we have yet to experience. So what will be required to respond positively to these new social changes? I would argue that it requires a mind-set that incorporates the three elements of a new national identity as articulated in this chapter. Compared to the rest of Japan, Okinawa is relatively unique by having a low rate of aging, a positive rate of population growth, and a majority of its residents in the workforce. In this sense, Okinawa's future prospects are bright, and this optimistic outlook has the potential to contribute enormously to the peace and prosperity of Japan as a whole.

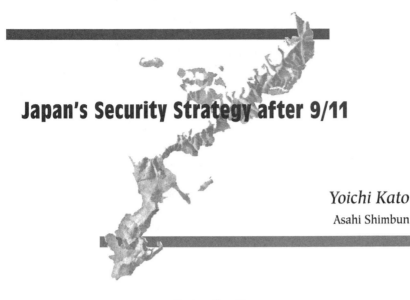

Japan's Security Strategy after 9/11

Yoichi Kato

Asahi Shimbun

Introduction

apan's national security strategy has been incrementally evolving ever since Japan restored its independence in 1952. Following the attacks of September 11, 2001, however, Japan has made two major policy decisions that represent a historical departure from the long-held security policy.

One was the decision to send Self-Defense Forces (SDF) to Iraq. It bears an unprecedented significance, not only because it indicates that Japan is now ready to assume the risks of sending troops to a region where the conflicts are not yet settled, but it also clearly manifests Japan's will to make use of the SDF as a diplomatic tool to shape the international strategic order.

The other significant move was the February 2004 revision of Japan's Foreign Exchange and Foreign Trade Control Law, the legal framework regulating foreign exchange transactions, so that Japan can unilaterally halt any remittance to North Korea if it so chooses. This is a clear indication that Japan has decided to take coercive measures in diplomacy. This is perhaps more significant than sending troops to Iraq.

Those two recent policy decisions show that Japan is, now more than ever, eager to take part in shaping the international strategic environment and order, instead of just focusing on preparation for potential invasion of its territory under the slogan of "exclusive defense." This change will have a direct impact on Japan's national interests.

Such new moves have brought about apprehension from neighboring states, including South Korea, that Japan may have moved beyond its defense policy limitation and into a more aggressive defense posture.

Japan's Strategic Vulnerability

One of the dominant factors for Japan's security strategy has been that its strategic vulnerability is distinctively high compared with neighboring countries and other major powers in the region. The following three factors constitute such vulnerability. The first factor is that most of Japan's elements of national power show either relative weakness or decline. Demography is the most evident case in point. Japan's population is predicted to start decreasing in 2007. Furthermore, it is widely known that Japan's dependence on petroleum imports is now more than ninety-nine percent of domestic consumption. The economy, being one of the social elements of national power, also exhibits weakness, without prospect of substantial recovery from the decade-long slump. The quality of political leadership can also be characterized as poor.

The second factor that dictates Japan's strategic vulnerability is globally extended business activities and globally engaged national interests, while the third involves the self-imposed restrictions on the tools of statecraft. Japan can only use diplomatic tools like "diplomatic persuasion" and "negotiation with incentives" to change the will or policy of other states. Japan has refrained from resorting to coercive means, such as the use or threat of force, based on the idea and spirit of Article 9 of its Constitution, which renounces the use of force as a means of settling international disputes.

Those three factors, mixed together, make Japan strategically highly vulnerable, because Japan's interests are extended globally without its own means to defend them, should such a need arise. Such strategic disadvantages are unlikely to disappear soon.

Countermeasures

There are basically two ways to deal with this issue of strategic vulnerability; one is to try to minimize vulnerability, and the other is to prevent the emergence of instability in the region and beyond.

To minimize Japanese vulnerability, national power has to be enhanced, the self-imposed restriction on coercive diplomacy has to be removed, or both. Some elements of national power are unchangeable, such as the poor reserve of natural resources in Japan. The trend of demographic downsizing can be reversed, but only with a substantial change of social structure, the way of life, and the mindset of the male population. This will be a lengthy, if not impossible, task. Addressing the social elements, like the economy and quality of political leadership, will also take time.

It seems easiest to expand the tools of statecraft to minimize Japan's vulnerability. Two recent policy decisions mentioned at the outset of this paper exemplify the expansion of policy choices: dispatch of the SDF to Iraq and revision of the Foreign Exchange and Foreign Trade Control Law to restrict remittances to North Korea. This approach will probably be more widely used in the future. Of course, the government will soon face the very difficult question of whether use of force should be legalized as a means of settling international disputes. This question directly leads to the politically controversial issue of amending Article 9 of the Constitution.

The other way to deal with the strategic vulnerability is to prevent the emergence of instability in the region or solve it at a low-intensity phase, should conflicts arise. As for the threat from North Korea, a set of military and diplomatic frameworks have already been established, the former being the alliance with the United States and the latter the Six Party Talks.

After 9/11, Japan perceived the threat of a terror attack on the sea lines of communication (SLOCs), which would disrupt the flow of both imports to and exports from Japan. Blocking the Malacca Strait, for example by sinking a large ship at a choke point, could inflict devastating damage on Japan's economy and also that of the region. To prevent such devastation, Japan has proposed an Ocean Peace Keeping (OPK) initiative. This is a good example of an approach to prevent conflicts or, failing that, to solve them at a low-intensity phase.

In May 2003, Japan's Minister of State for Defense Shigeru Ishiba explained the idea in detail at the Shangri-La Dialogue, an annual defense ministers' meeting in Singapore. According to his explanation, each participating state would contribute its own naval assets and capabilities to form a multilateral, international framework for policing the open waters of the Asia-Pacific region, especially in Southeast Asia, where both piracy and terrorist attacks have recently increased to an alarming level. Contributing Japanese P-3C aircraft from the Air SDF for surveillance has already been discussed by Japanese experts as a potential way for Japan to participate.

Strategic Shift and Challenges

To deal with post-9/11 threats, Japan has already decided to review its defense posture to address new threats like ballistic missiles and terrorist attacks. The plan, authorized by the Cabinet in December 2003, calls for a change from the long-held commitment to possessing minimum necessary defense capabilities to a new threat-based approach. It discusses transforming the SDF into more agile and multipurpose forces to defend Japan from the new threats and carry out other missions like anti-proliferation, humanitarian assistance, and peacekeeping.

This plan does not mention China at all, but the Japan Defense Agency (JDA) and the SDF regard China as a "potential problem for Japan." They are troubled by the constant increase of China's defense budget. By 2004, it had been growing more than ten percent for sixteen consecutive years. According to JDA analysis, the Chinese military is transforming from a quantity-focused to a quality-focused force and is modernizing the navy and air force in particular by procuring new weapon systems from Russia. The JDA is most concerned that Japan's SLOCs might come under the influence of China's expanded military capability. To counter such potential moves by China, some ideas have started to materialize within the Japanese government to strengthen defense capabilities along the island chain from Kyushu to Okinawa.

Japan's vital interest in the region should be to prevent the emergence of a hostile hegemon, and it shares this interest with the United States. As a junior alliance partner lacking the option of using force as a means to settle international disputes, however, Japan should pursue the following policy:

- Enhance the U.S.-Japan Security Alliance
- Diversify diplomatic tools and options
- Hedge against a weakening of the U.S.-Japan Security Alliance

Japan faces challenges in pursuing such a policy: the lack of strategic dialogue between the U.S. and Japan; incomplete regional reconciliation, especially with China and the Koreas; and the need for a clearly defined regional interest and strategic order.

For Japan to make a shift in its national security strategy, it must engage in a substantial strategic dialogue with the United States. Japan has to ensure that such a shift would not contradict or compromise the existing security arrangement and future planning of the alliance with the United States. Actual dialogue regarding strategy has not, however, been fully conducted. The U.S.-Japan Joint Declaration on Security, signed by Prime Minister Ryutaro Hashimoto and President Bill Clinton in 1996, stipulates that both governments will continue to consult closely on defense policies and military postures, including the U.S. force structure in Japan. Regardless, there has been no such consultation on U.S. force structure in Japan made public in the last seven years.

After 9/11, a new framework for strategic dialogue, dubbed the Defense Policy Review Initiative (DPRI), was established between the two governments. It is a forum for the exchange of views on strategy and policy, but all the discussions have thus far been kept secret from the public and its accomplishments are not yet clear.

For Japan to expand its security role in the region, it must have the understanding if not the positive support of neighboring countries. Even though the situation is slowly changing, it is still very common to see alarming reactions from China and the Koreas whenever Japan starts new initiatives involving role expansion of the SDF. This is due to the unsettled historical issues with those countries. Regardless of how often Japan claims that it has implemented enough measures that address the issue, as long as Japan's neighbors are not satisfied and do not stop casting doubts on Japan's strategic intentions, it will be very hard for Japan to successfully implement any of the new security initiatives. In this regard, Prime Minister Junichiro Koizumi's repeated visits to Yasukuni Shrine where war criminals from World War II are enshrined do not help Japan proceed with any new security initiatives.

Another obstacle to regional understanding and support for Japan's new security initiatives is Japan's lack of a clear articulation of its national interests and security strategy. Even the JDA's Defense White Paper and the Ministry of Foreign Affairs' Diplomatic Blue Book do not contain any definition of Japan's national interests or a comprehensive national security strategy. This lack of explanation invites regional doubts regarding Japan's strategic intentions.

U.S. Strategy in the Asia-Pacific:
Alliances and Coalitions, Wheels and Webs

Mike M. Mochizuki

George Washington University

I n their November 2002 report to Prime Minister Junichiro Koizumi, a blue ribbon panel on Japan's foreign policy strategy for the twenty-first century echoed the common criticism that the United States is too unilateral in its foreign policy. This advisory group stated that "of particular concern is the fact that, during the 1990s, the United States tended to incline away from strong support for the international 'public purpose' and toward action based on simplistic self-interest."[1]

America's temptation to act unilaterally is not all that surprising. Its relative power and influence are unprecedented in modern history. Imperial Britain of the nineteenth century pales in comparison with the United States in the early twenty-first century. The United States' remarkable economic revival in the 1990s put to rest the notion that Japan might supercede America and that the new century would be a Pacific Century. And despite China's rapid economic ascendancy, its military capabilities lag far behind that of the United States and the military technology gap between the two does not appear to be closing — indeed it might even be widening. Moreover, the social and political contradictions of China's economic modernization suggest that it would be misguided to extrapolate China's current growth rates far into the future. America's unilateral temptation, however, is not simply a matter of relative power. It has its roots in American national identity and character: an exceptional country suspicious of "entangling alliances," impatient with diplomacy, and prone to see the world through a transformative lens with the United States as the global beacon of democracy and enlightenment.

■══

Alliances Versus Ad Hoc Coalitions

As the recent experiences from Iraq to North Korea have demonstrated, however, even the sole superpower cannot pursue its international agenda alone. The United States needs the support (or at least acquiescence) of other states to legitimate its actions, to gain international leverage, to execute military operations, and to share the financial and human costs of its global strategy. Indeed as Joseph Nye has argued, globalization and technological developments have produced a paradox of American power: even as American power is unprecedented and unchallenged, the United States needs the support of other countries and the international community more than ever before.[2] But how that support should be mobilized and sustained remains an open question.

Although during the Cold War, formal alliances functioned effectively in support of America's international agenda of containing international communism, some now argue that the age of alliances has come to an end. According to this view, the collapse of the Soviet Union removed the overriding geopolitical rationale that kept the Western alliance coherent, and the expansion of NATO (North Atlantic Treaty Organization) to save NATO will only make the alliance more incoherent. France and Germany's active effort to thwart U.S. policy toward Iraq demonstrates how problematic the trans-Atlantic alliance has become. In observing the rift between America and what Secretary of Defense Donald Rumsfeld has indignantly called the "old Europe," Rajan Menon draws the following conclusion:

> America will revert to a pattern it has followed for most of
> its history, operating in the world without fixed, long-term
> alliances and pursuing its interests and safeguarding its
> security in cooperation with a range of partners. This is all
> to the good: the problems of diplomacy and national security
> are variegated, states (and organizations) that are useful and
> appropriate for the pursuit of one goal will not necessarily
> be the ones best suited for another. In a world that presents
> threats and opportunities wholly different from those
> encountered during the Cold War, the United States will be
> best served by agile and creative statecraft that looks beyond
> — but does not exclude—traditional friends and solutions, and
> that musters alignments and coalitions that vary according to
> the context.[3]

To use the metaphor invoked by Richard Haass, the United States can best play the role of global sheriff by mobilizing his ad hoc posse ("coalition of the willing") to deal with specific international challenges.

Relying primarily on formal alliances and international organizations will only impede prompt and effective action.[4]

But other analysts are unwilling to sound the death knell for alliances. For example, John Ikenberry argues that alliances are more than inter-state groupings to counter common external threats. Alliances also work to bind the member states together by providing reassurances about the future and an institutionalized mechanism for consultations. By being formally allied to the United States, states are able to constrain American unilateral behavior and gain an opportunity to voice their interests and preferences *vis à vis* the United States — and ultimately to shape U.S. policy. From the U.S. perspective, rather than impeding American policy, formal alliance arrangements can encourage allied nations to cooperate more actively with the United States. Because allies are reassured about American behavior and because they have a voice in determining collective policy, they will be much more energetic in backing a course of international action led by the United States.[5] Moreover, formal alliances allow the United States to maintain a quasi-permanent military presence overseas. This forward deployment of U.S. forces not only facilitates American military operations (whether they are conducted alone or with the active participation of allied states), but also helps to discourage regional orders that might exclude the United States or that might be antithetical to American basic interests. Some also argue that the U.S. overseas military presence through its geopolitical reassurance function mitigates the emergence of vexing security dilemmas in both Europe and East Asia.

So how do these contrasting views of formal alliances fare in the context of the Asia-Pacific region? The irony of the last decade is that despite the purported strong historical and cultural ties that bind together America and Europe, the trans-Atlantic alliance appears more troubled than America's alliances across the Pacific (with the notable exception of the U.S.-South Korea alliance). The split over Iraq policy between the United States and Britain on the one hand, and France, Germany, and Belgium on the other, may be just the tip of the iceberg. The multi-decade process of European integration may finally be bearing fruit by creating another center of global power that can serve as a counterweight to the United States.[6]

The situation in the Asia-Pacific region is very different. First, although the fall of the Berlin Wall symbolized the end of the Cold War in Europe, the conflicts that emerged in the context of the Cold War remain in East Asia. Korea continues to be divided with little progress toward national reconciliation, and Taiwan is still a contentious issue in U.S.-China relations. Either could become a military flashpoint. It goes without saying that a resolution of the Korea and Taiwan questions would have profound implications for the U.S. alliance network across the Pacific. But as for now, both Korea and Taiwan provide a persuasive strategic rationale for existing alliance arrangements. Second, despite the growth of intra-regional trade and the inauguration of various multilateral regional institutions and dialogues, East Asia lags far behind Europe in developing a regional identity that could provide the foundation for countering the United States.[7] Asia lacks a partnership analogous to the Franco-German relationship which served as the core of European integration. Historical mistrust still hampers the development of such partnerships between Japan and South Korea and between Japan and China. Finally, while Russia is formally outside NATO, the impact of Russia on NATO's coherence or incoherence is rather minimal. Whereas Russia may not matter that much for the geopolitics and geoeconomics of Europe, China certainly matters a great deal for East Asia. The rise of China can pose for other states in the region the difficult choice between balancing against or bandwagoning with Chinese power. At least for the time being, the U.S. alliance system and forward military deployments alleviate the need to make such a strategic choice about China. Therefore, on balance, the centripetal forces behind the U.S. alliance relationships in the Asia-Pacific appear stronger than the centrifugal forces that could drive the alliances apart.

But how does the United States view its alliances in the region relative to other forms of international cooperation (e.g. emerging partnerships, ad hoc coalitions of the willing, and various multilateral processes and dialogues)? Much depends on what the United States sees as the salient international challenges at any given point in time.

Before the terrorist attacks on September 11, 2001, the Bush administration tended to see the world in classic realist terms with a focus on great power relations and the relative distribution of power. The way to prevent great power conflicts was not to forge arms control or other cooperative security arrangements with would-be competitors, but to ensure American political-military supremacy thereby dissuading such potential competitors from seeking to challenge the United States in the first place. A key U.S. strategic objective was to prevent any critical region of the world from being dominated by a hostile power.[8]

The application of this mind-set to the Asia-Pacific region meant a focus on China as a possible strategic competitor and Japan as a key ally in countering the rise of Chinese power. The Bush administration in the pre-September 11 period was never explicit about how Japan might be harnessed in an American effort to constrain China's growing power. Perhaps they thought that such an explicit strategy would be counterproductive, premature, and unnecessary. Nevertheless, those associated with the Bush presidential campaign openly criticized the

Clinton administration's policy of "constructing a strategic partnership with China" and its poor treatment of Japan as an ally when President Clinton bypassed Japan on his way to China. They also seemed to disagree with Henry Kissinger's notion that the United States should maintain a delicate balance between Chinese and Japanese power.

In practice, the Bush administration has sought to build on, rather than reject, the legacy of the Clinton administration regarding security relations with Japan. The new Guidelines for U.S.-Japan Defense Cooperation adopted in 1997 offered the potential of Japan supporting the United States militarily in various contingencies — even those involving China and Taiwan. Rather than excluding Taiwan from the bilateral defense guidelines, Tokyo adhered to a policy of military ambiguity. Japanese cooperation with the United States on ballistic missile defense research offered another avenue for Japan to work with the U.S. on constraining China.

Although Japan may serve as a linchpin of U.S. strategy in the Asia-Pacific region, it was by no means sufficient for American objectives. For example, the U.S. Defense Department's 2001 *Quadrennial Defense Review Report* highlighted the East Asia littoral (which spans from south of Japan through Australia and into the Bay of Bengal) as a critical and potentially volatile region because of major power transitions, national and transnational extremist movements, possible failed states, and the spread of weapons of mass destruction. But meeting these security challenges would be difficult even for the sole superpower, because the geographic distances were so great and the United States had fewer overseas bases and access arrangements to facilitate the projection of U.S. military power. These shortcomings led defense officials to look beyond traditional formal alliances to buttress American capabilities.

Alliances and Coalitions in the Post-September 11 World

September 11 prompted a major reorientation in U.S. strategy. In its September 2002 National Security Strategy report, the Bush administration argued that the gravest danger to the United States and global security did not come from "conquering states" that mobilized "great armies and great industrial capabilities."[9] The salient threats now came from terrorists, rogue states, and failing or weak states; and these threats were especially ominous because they "lie at the crossroads of radicalism and technology." But the Bush administration also saw the present era as a time of great opportunity. The United States "possesses unprecedented — and unequaled—strength and influence in the world," the ideas of freedom and equality have defeated and discredited "destructive totalitarianism," and "the common dangers of terrorist violence and chaos" facilitate cooperation with the "main centers of global power." Several noteworthy points emerged from this strategic reorientation.

First, the 2002 strategy report stressed that reactive actions such as deterrence and retaliation were inadequate to counter threats that derived from the marriage of radicalism and technology. In making the case for pre-emptive military action, the report alluded to international law which "for centuries... recognized that nations need not suffer an attack before they can lawfully take action to defend themselves against forces that present an imminent danger of attack." The Bush administration argued that traditional deterrence is unlikely to work against rogue states, because their leaders are "more willing to take risks, gambling with the lives of their people, and the wealth of their nations." And the potential use of weapons of mass destruction has magnified the danger from terrorists and rogue states. Since "the greater the threat, the greater is the risk of inaction," the United States "will, if necessary, act pre-emptively." But as Brookings Institution critics of the Bush strategy have noted, this new doctrine of pre-emption does not specify the ultimate aim of such action — that is, whether it is simply to eliminate the threatening capabilities of rogue states or to overthrow the rogue regimes themselves.[10]

Second, the post-September 11 Bush strategy highlighted the possibility of cooperation among the great powers while downplaying the competitive aspects. In his cover letter to the September 2002 strategy report, President Bush states that "we will preserve the peace by building good relations among the great powers." He goes on to write: "Today, the international community has the best chance since the rise of the nation-state in the seventeenth century to build a world where great powers compete in peace instead of continually prepare for war. Today, the world's great powers find ourselves on the same side — united by common dangers of terrorist violence and chaos. The United States will build on these common interests to promote global security. We are also increasingly united by common values." The Bush strategy never offers a clear definition of a "great power," but it does cite Russia, India, and China as examples of great powers with which increasing cooperation might be possible.

In contrast to the Bush presidential campaign and the first phase of the Bush presidency, gone are the references to China as a "strategic competitor" or to the need to consider containing China. The Bush strategy after September 11 unequivocally declares that the United States welcomes "the emergence of a strong, peaceful, and prosperous China" and "seeks a constructive relationship with a changing China." It emphasizes that the U.S. and China have been cooperating in the war on terrorism and in the promotion of stability on the Korean Peninsula.

As Michael Swaine notes in his chapter, tensions could re-emerge in Sino-American relations (especially over Taiwan), but at least for now this bilateral relationship appears to be as good as it has been ever been since the 1989 Tiananmen massacre — some might even say since normalization in the late 1970s. Therefore, the notion of actively enlisting Japan in a balancing strategy against a rising China has much less resonance than before September 11.

Finally, the Bush strategy mentions the need to act unilaterally in some instances: "While the United States will constantly strive to enlist the support of the international community, we will not hesitate to act alone, if necessary, to exercise our right of self-defense by acting pre-emptively against such terrorists, to prevent them from doing harm against our people and our country." The last page of the strategy report proclaims that "in exercising our leadership, we will respect the values, judgment, and interests of our friends and partners. Still, we will be prepared to act apart when our interests and unique responsibilities require." Although much has been made of this statement about unilateral action, even the Clinton administration reserved this option for the United States. In its 1999 strategy report, the Clinton administration noted that "we must always be prepared to act alone when that is our most advantageous course, or when we have no alternative."[11]

Indeed the difference between Bush and Clinton may be more one of emphasis than of kind. The 1999 Clinton strategy report argued that "many of our security objectives are best achieved — or can only be achieved — by leveraging our influence and capabilities through international organizations, our alliances, or as a leader of an ad hoc coalition formed around a specific objective." In the cover letter to his strategy report, President Bush echoes this theme: "We are ... guided by the conviction that no nation can build a safer, better world alone. Alliances and multilateral institutions can multiply the strength of freedom-loving nations." In fact, even in its embrace of a pre-emption doctrine, the Bush strategy saw the need to work with allies "to form a common assessment of the most dangerous threats." In addition to coordinating intelligence capabilities, the United States would need the help of other states "to conduct rapid and precise" military operations over long distances. Therefore, the real debate in the United States is not about unilateral versus collective action, but about the relative emphasis that should be placed on international organizations, alliances, and ad hoc coalitions of the willing in pursuing strategic objectives. For the United States, international organizations and alliances are rarely ends in themselves. They are seen more as tools of foreign policy. They will be emphasized when they facilitate American action, and they will be downplayed or even circumvented when they impede such action.

Implications for the Asia-Pacific

September 11 shifted America's strategic focus away from China as a potential geopolitical competitor to terrorism, rogue states, and the proliferation of weapons of mass destruction. With the possibility of a Cold War between the United States and China on hold for the time being, the salient issues for U.S. allies and partners in the Asia-Pacific region now involve the operations in Afghanistan and Iraq, the North Korean nuclear problem, and the campaign against terrorism in Southeast Asia.

AFGHANISTAN AND IRAQ

Regarding both Afghanistan and Iraq, the United States found its Pacific allies to be quite supportive. In terms of Afghanistan, Australia invoked for the first time its fifty-year old alliance treaty with the United States to support the U.S. military operation there by deploying 1,500 military personnel including four fighter aircraft, two maritime patrol, and two refueling aircraft, Special Forces, three frigates, and one amphibious command ship. Japan passed in October 2001 its Anti-Terrorism Special Measures Law which enabled the deployment of Self-Defense Force (SDF) vessels to refuel American and British naval ships in the Indian Ocean, the use of SDF aircraft to provide transportation support for U.S. forces, and the eventual dispatch of an Aegis-equipped destroyer to the Indian Ocean.[12] South Korea sent Air Force and Navy airlift fleet groups as well as a medical support unit to assist "Operation Enduring Freedom" against Afghanistan.[13]

Even on the more controversial war against Iraq, U.S. allies in the Pacific did not go the way of France and Germany. Australia supported the Bush administration diplomatically and sent naval units to help enforce UN Security Council sanctions against Iraq. In July 2003, Australia decided to participate in the postwar reconstruction of Iraq by initiating Operation Catalyst which involves about 800 personnel. Despite the tensions in U.S.-South Korea relations after the death of two Korean junior high school students in a traffic accident involving two U.S. servicemen, South Korean President Roh Moo-hyun affirmed the importance of the U.S.-South Korea alliance, proclaimed his support of coalition forces in Iraq, and deployed a construction engineering group and a medical support group of 675 personnel for humanitarian support and relief activities in postwar Iraq. The Roh government has also decided to send additional forces to postwar Iraq. Despite strong public skepticism (if not downright opposition) to the U.S.-led war against Iraq, the Japanese government backed the United States publicly and extended its rear-area logistical support of American military operations. Moreover, Japan passed legislation regarding the postwar reconstruction of Iraq that would permit the deployment of ground forces to Iraq, and Prime Minister Koizumi has followed through by dispatching forces.

What explains this support for the United States? The existence of long-term and institutionalized alliance relationships did facilitate this support, but such an explanation is insufficient. The split in NATO over Iraq demonstrates that alliance institutions are not enough to mobilize support for a controversial U.S. policy. More was at work in the Asia-Pacific context. For Australia, its historical identity as part of an Anglo-American community as well as the presence of a conservative government probably helped to steer the country behind the United States. But a critical factor was certainly the October 2002 Bali terrorist bombings. For both South Korea and Japan, it appears that the desire to have a voice *vis à vis* the United States on North Korea policy may have been central to their calculations. If these countries had gone the way of France and Germany in defiantly opposing the United States on Iraq, it would be much more difficult to press their respective interests and perspectives regarding the North Korea issue. Nevertheless, the South Korean and Japanese governments' support of the Bush administration on Iraq is tenuous. The recent political difficulties of President Roh exacerbate his dilemma between winning America's favor by deploying combat forces to Iraq versus responding to his core anti-war constituents. For Japan, the cost of supporting Bush on Iraq has been modest both in terms of treasure and life so far. Japan's financial contribution to both Operation Enduring Freedom and Operation Iraqi Freedom is a far cry from the $13 billion contribution to Desert Shield and Desert Storm. But Japanese casualties after a ground force deployment in Iraq could trigger a strong political backlash against both Prime Minister Koizumi and the United States.

The Australian, Japanese, and South Korean support of operations against Iraq also needs to be put in perspective. While their support was certainly welcomed by the Bush administration, their military role has been minimal compared to the United Kingdom. None of these three allies have the capability to project military power overseas like the United States — or even Britain and France. Moreover, as Sheldon Simon has recently argued, the technological gap between U.S. forces on the one hand, and those of its formal allies in the Asia-Pacific on the other hand, impedes efficient and effective interactions in actual military contingencies.[14]

NORTH KOREA

Despite concerns that the United States will adopt a pre-emptive policy against North Korea as it did against Iraq, the Bush administration has gradually moved toward a multilateral strategy of maximizing diplomatic pressure against North Korea in hopes that Pyongyang will agree to a verifiable and irreversible dismantling of its nuclear weapons program. Bush's multilateral approach goes beyond its embrace of the Six Party Talks convened by China. In May 2003, President Bush launched the Proliferation Security Initiative (PSI) as a multinational effort to prevent the proliferation of weapons of mass destruction and their delivery systems by strengthening trade inspections, sharing information about suspicious shipments, and increasing searches and seizures of ships, planes, and vehicles that could be smuggling weapons of mass destruction (WMD) and their delivery capabilities. The eleven inaugural members of this initiative are Australia, France, the United Kingdom, Germany, Italy, Japan, the Netherlands, Poland, Portugal, Spain, and the United States. What is remarkable about this coalition is the inclusion of both France and Germany — the staunch opponents of Bush on Iraq — and the absence of South Korea. PSI does not explicitly target specific countries, but the Bush administration certainly had North Korea in mind.

If the strategy of multilateral pressure succeeds in compelling North Korea to back down, then the Bush administration appears to be willing to provide security assurances to North Korea, lift sanctions and facilitate economic aid, and normalize relations. Although Washington, Seoul, and Tokyo have different perspectives and priorities regarding North Korea, they have managed to minimize public disagreements about policy through the Trilateral Coordination and Oversight Group (TCOG) consultative mechanism. But the real test of this virtual alliance will come if the multilateral talks convened by China fail to yield sufficient progress and North Korea moves further along the path to becoming an unambiguous nuclear weapons state.

South Korea's priority on avoiding both war and a North Korean collapse could put Seoul and Washington at odds if the latter decided to move toward a tight containment and squeezing strategy — even while forgoing the military pre-emption option. Thus far, South Korean economic aid to North Korea that was initiated as part of President Kim Dae-jung's "Sunshine Policy" has been largely unconditional. And South Korea appears reluctant to join the PSI. How willing would the South Koreans be about turning off this aid as part of a U.S.-led squeezing strategy? Would fears of provoking North Korea steer South Korea toward China, thereby further weakening the already troubled U.S.-South Korea alliance? Much will depend on domestic political developments in South Korea which are becoming murkier by the day.

On the face of it, Japan appears more supportive of a hardline U.S. policy toward North Korea because of the Japanese public's increasing animosity toward North Korea over the abduction issue. Japan has already terminated aid to North Korea except for modest humanitarian assistance, and it has become more willing to force inspections and delays of North Korean ships that enter Japanese ports. The Koizumi government seems to be preparing for a containment strategy by considering a ban on all financial remittances to North Korea via Japanese financial institutions, restricting exchanges of people between Japan and North Korea and denying North Korean crews permission to disembark at Japanese ports, and supporting a UN Security Council resolution that denounces North Korea and mandates economic sanctions. But would Japan be willing to participate in a naval quarantine of North Korea or even to stop all shipping between Japan and North Korea?

For the United States, the North Korean issue reveals most sharply the constraints on unilateral action. The U.S.-South Korea and U.S.-Japan alliances function not simply as tools of U.S. policy, but as institutions that can restrain U.S. policy. How well South Korea and Japan will use what John Ikenberry refers to as their "voicing opportunities" remains to be seen.

Finally, a resolution of the Korean question (either through North-South reconciliation or a collapse of the North Korean regime) will prompt major adjustments in both the U.S.-South Korea and U.S.-Japan alliances. The latter alliance has already moved toward refocusing security cooperation beyond a Korean contingency. Nevertheless, a post-Korean conflict security environment is likely to compel a major restructuring (and even reduction) of U.S. forces in Japan, especially the Marines in Okinawa. The impact on U.S. forces in Korea and the U.S.-South Korea alliance is likely to be even greater. The American preference will probably be to maintain the bilateral alliance and deploy modest air and naval (and possibly Marine) units in Korea while acquiescing to the removal of most the ground forces. But how a reconciled or reunited Korea would respond to such an option is uncertain. Much will depend on Korean domestic politics as well as the state of Korea's political relations with China, Japan, and the United States.

CAMPAIGN AGAINST TERRORISM IN SOUTHEAST ASIA

Although Southeast Asia has been viewed as the second front in the war against terrorism, the Bali terrorist bombings of October 2002 demonstrated that this struggle can be just as lethal as in the first front. Although the United States lacks robust security alliances comparable to those with Japan, Australia, and South Korea in Southeast Asia, it has worked to enhance cooperation with various states in the region in identifying and countering terrorist threats.

The three closest U.S. security partners in the region are Singapore, Thailand, and the Philippines. The Singaporean military is the most advanced of the three countries and has the technological capability to interact relatively well with U.S. forces. The uncovering of a significant radical Islamic network in the city-state with the objective of inciting communal unrest has mobilized Singapore to be vigilant and more forthcoming about intelligence sharing about possible terrorist activities. Compared to Singapore, Thailand's security capabilities lag far behind in technological sophistication, and domestic political concerns inhibit more energetic cooperation with the United States to counter terrorism. Nevertheless, Thailand has hosted the annual Cobra Gold multilateral military exercises involving U.S. and Southeast Asian forces, and in 2002 these exercises focused on anti-terrorism as well as peacekeeping and drug interdiction. Despite the historic problems in the U.S.-Philippines security relationship, Manila has been a strong supporter of the United States against both Afghanistan and Iraq. And in the wake of September 11, the Philippines has invited the United States to train and equip its military. The most prominent example is the Balikatan training exercise in Mindanao during which U.S. forces worked to enhance interoperability with Filipino counterparts in anti-terrorist missions.

Bilateral security cooperation, however, is by no means adequate to meet the challenge of transnational terrorist threats that have penetrated Indonesia, Malaysia, the Philippines, and Singapore. Dealing with terrorist threats requires region-wide coordination among law enforcement, financial, intelligence, and military authorities. Concerns about indigenous Islamic populations in some states like Malaysia and Indonesia have restrained ASEAN from moving more quickly in developing effective region-wide mechanisms to combat terrorism. Nevertheless, the ASEAN states have agreed to share intelligence and coordinate anti-terror laws, and the United States is helping out by providing financial and technical assistance to police, customs, and finance officials in the region. Insofar as the root of the problem is social, economic, and political, and there are no rogue states that are to be toppled with force, U.S. military power has much less of a role to play compared to the Middle East. But to the extent that special military operations might be necessary to attack terrorist cells, rescue hostages, interdict shipments of contraband, and prevent piracy, the United States is likely to seek better military access in Southeast Asia and training grounds closer to the region.

What implications does this security challenge in Southeast Asia have for U.S. formal alliances in the Pacific? Although U.S. bases in Northeast Asia could provide good departure points for security missions in Southeast Asia, there will be a strong pull to deploy and train more U.S. forces southward. And if the Korean problem winds down and the so-called southern "arc of crisis" becomes the key security problem for the United States, a radical restructuring of U.S. overseas troop deployments appears highly probable. Such a development may ultimately blur the line between the formal alliances that were forged during the Cold War and the new partnerships that are being nurtured in the war against terrorism.

Wheels and Webs

Despite predictions that the era of U.S. alliances is about to end and criticisms that the United States has a propensity toward unilateralism, what is remarkable about the Asia-Pacific region is how critical formal alliances still are for U.S. strategy and how interested the United States is in cooperating with other states (whether allies or partners) to meet the salient security threats. What is equally remarkable is the degree to which the Bush administration has embraced multilateral processes and forums (e.g. TCOG, the Six Party Talks, PSI, APEC, and ARF) to promote its security agenda in the region.

So what implications does this approach have for the future regional security order? The United States will certainly continue to strengthen its formal bilateral alliances in the Asia-Pacific, especially that with Japan. In its proposals for restructuring U.S. forces in Japan as part of its military transformation initiative, the Pentagon has clearly suggested that it now views the U.S.-Japan security relationship as a global, not just a regional, alliance. By adopting a new security strategy that makes improving the international security environment one of the key missions of the SDF, Japan in turn has expressed its willingness to deepen defense cooperation with the United States and to enhance the interoperability of U.S. and Japanese forces. In February 2005, the United States and Japan invigorated the alliance by articulating common strategic objectives (see Appendix).

Over the last decade, however, the United States also appears to be moving gradually beyond the old "hub and spokes" model of its alliance network in the Asia-Pacific. Traditionally, this network of bilateral alliances provided the U.S. with the geopolitical advantage of making relations between the U.S. and its Asian allies and partners stronger than relations *among* its Asian allies and partners. But in the post-9/11 world, such a "divide and rule" approach has become much less tenable. At a minimum, the United States probably desires to transform the "hub and spokes" into a fully formed wheel in which security cooperation *among* U.S. allies is enhanced.[15] Japan-Australia and Japan-South Korea bilateral dialogues and security cooperation are key steps in this wheel formation. But as this paper has argued, the U.S. is also looking beyond formal alliances for security-related partnerships.

There is much debate about what kind of regional security architecture should be constructed and what kind of architecture is possible. Some argue for a "concert of the major powers in Asia" (the U.S., China, Japan, Russia, and India), while others advocate the development of a more inclusive regional security community that contains smaller states as well as the great powers. More pessimistic analysts predict the emergence of a bipolar competitive order between the United States and China with the other states in the region struggling about which side to choose. But what may in fact be emerging is a regional environment that is much less tidy than security architects might imagine. In what seems to be a region trying to catch up in institution building, the Asia-Pacific has witnessed in recent years a flourishing of multilateral forums, dialogues, and processes on a variety of issues. At this point, skeptics are correct in pointing out that this activity has yet to produce meaningful multilateral regimes that can truly regulate the behavior of member states and solve difficult international security issues. But one should not underestimate their future potential, because this activity rests upon a profound integrative transformation of the regional economy and is motivated by a strong desire to avoid isolation and to counter potential threats. All of the key states in the region, including the United States, Japan, and China, are in the business of network building — both formal and informal. Some of these emerging networks have the United States as a central member, others exclude the United States. But the collective outcome of this activity is the emergence of a region with interlocking networks.

For this kind of Asia-Pacific region, traditional realist notions of a parsimonious balance of power scheme may become less relevant. The states in the region are instead becoming entangled in an organic web of their own making with the ultimate effect of constraining their behavior and even promoting inter-state cooperation. In such a web-like order, as Harry Harding has argued, the region may be appropriately characterized as a "multi-nodal" rather than a "multipolar" one. Whereas multipolarity connotes a situation in which the poles repel each other, "multi-nodality" defines a situation in which different units (or nodes) try to attract others into their network.

This notion can be applied to the "Okinawa question." Thus far, Okinawa's attractiveness in the contemporary world of international politics has been primarily military. It has served well as a major hub of U.S. military operations in the Pacific and even beyond. And with continuing tensions in the Korean Peninsula and the potential for a Taiwan contingency, this military function is unlikely to disappear. But one cannot deny that the military attractiveness of Okinawa for the United States has also distorted the island prefecture's economic development (see chapter by Oshiro). The challenge facing Okinawa and the U.S.-Japan Security Alliance today is how to supplement the military hub Okinawa with an Okinawa that can become one of the dynamic nodes of the Asia-Pacific economy. To do so, Okinawa must become its own web weaver as well, and the United States and Japan must create a modicum of space for Okinawa to do so. Interestingly, the recent moves to strengthen U.S.-Japan defense cooperation during both global and regional security contingencies offer an excellent opportunity to explore creative ways for reducing the "quasi-permanent" U.S. military presence on Okinawa and to chart a more prosperous future for this island prefecture.

[1] Taigai Kankei Tasuku Foosu, *21 Seiki Nihon Gaiko no Kihon Senryaku: Aratana Jidai, Aratana Bijon, Aratana Gaiko* (Basic strategies for Japan's foreign policy in the 21st century: new era, new vision, new diplomacy), 28 November 2002.

[2] Joseph S. Nye, Jr., *The Paradox of American Power: Why the World's Only Superpower Can't Go It Alone*, Oxford University Press, 2002.

[3] Rajan Menon, "The End of Alliances," *World Policy Journal,* Summer 2003.

[4] Richard Haass, *The Reluctant Sheriff: The United States after the Cold War*, Council on Foreign Relations, New York, 1997.

[5] G. John Ikenberry, "America's Alliances in the Age of Unipolarity" (unpublished paper, January 2003).

[6] Charles A. Kupchan, *The End of the American Era: U.S. Foreign Policy and the Geopolitics of the Twenty-First Century*, Alfred A. Knopf, 2002, pp.119–159.

[7] Some of these multilateral regional institutions and dialogues are the Asia-Pacific Economic Cooperation (APEC) forum, the ASEAN (Association of Southeast Asian Nations) Regional Forum, the ASEAN Plus Three (China, Japan, and South Korea), the Northeast Asia Cooperation Dialogue, and the North Pacific (NORPAC) dialogue.

[8] See for example the 2001 *Quadrennial Defense Review Report*. Although this document was released after the September 11 terrorist attacks, much of it was drafted before the attacks.

[9] *The National Security Strategy of the United States of America*, September 2002.

[10] Michael O'Hanlon, Susan E. Rice, and James B. Steinberg, "The New National Security Strategy and Pre-emption," *The Brookings Institution Policy Brief #113*, January 2003.

[11] The White House, *A New National Security Strategy for a New Century*, December 1999, pp.4–5.

[12] Charles E. Morrison (ed.), *Asia Pacific Security Outlook 2003*, Japan Center for International Exchange, 2003, pp.27 and 83.

[13] Ministry of National Defense [of the ROK], *ROK-US Alliance and USFK*, June 2003, p.45.

[14] Sheldon Simon, "Theater Security Cooperation in the U.S. Pacific Command: An Assessment and Projection," *NBR Analysis* Vol. 14, No. 2, August 2003.

[15] Dennis C. Blair and John T. Hanley, Jr, "From Wheels to Webs: Reconstructing Asia-Pacific Security Arrangements," *The Washington Quarterly* Vol. 24, No. 1, Winter 2001, pp.7–17.

Military Bases and Economic Development in Okinawa

Implementing the SACO (Special Action Committee on Okinawa) and Revising the SOFA (Status of Forces Agreement)

Hisayoshi Ina
Nihon Keizai Shimbun

Why the SOFA and the SACO?

T he Okinawa military base issue grabbed nationwide attention in Japan following the 1995 rape of a primary school student by U.S. servicemen in Okinawa. Growing discontent over the U.S.-Japan Status of Forces Agreement (SOFA), whereby American soldiers suspected of criminal activity are not handed over to Japanese authorities until an indictment is made by the Public Prosecutor's Office, led to a Joint Committee agreement by the American and Japanese governments to improve the administration of the SOFA. In the Joint Committee agreement, it was decided that in specific cases of heinous crimes like murder or rape, the United States would consider sympathetically any Japanese request concerning the detention of a suspect prior to an indictment made by Japan.

Okinawan discontent was not solely related to the bilateral SOFA. What was being questioned was the fact that seventy-five percent of the total land used exclusively by the U.S. military in Japan is concentrated within Okinawa. There was concern that if this problem was not addressed, it would destabilize the U.S.-Japan Security Treaty. As a result, the Special Action Committee on Okinawa (SACO) was formed to begin the consultative process. In April 1996, the SACO Interim Report — including an agreement for the return of the U.S. Marine Corps' Futenma Air Station — was presented, and in December, the SACO Final Report (See Appendix) was released.

The two issues are related to attempts aimed at reducing the bases' burden on Okinawa. This problem, however, has not been resolved.

While the voices of those demanding a revision of the SOFA remain strong, the environment for bilateral negotiation between Japan and the U.S. is not yet conducive to agreement. While the base streamlining mentioned in the SACO Final Report is underway, the relocation of Futenma, with its symbolic ramifications, is not progressing. This is why resolving the fifteen-year time limit issue raised in Okinawa Governor Keiichi Inamine's election promise is essential.

What is required to lighten the burden of the bases as mentioned in the SACO agreement? Protest and simply making demands on the U.S. will have limited effect. Instead, there must be negotiation between Japan and the U.S. Therefore, Japan must examine the U.S.-Japan Security Alliance and cultivate an environment more fit for change.

The SOFA Resulting from a Conflict in Sovereignty

What, generally, is a Status of Forces Agreement or SOFA? The history of such agreements is relatively recent, with the necessity for them arising after World War I. Until then, armed forces, which represent the essence of a country's sovereignty, were not stationed in foreign countries except as occupying powers.

When an occupying army is present in a country, the actions of its troops are not subject to that country's restrictions. However, during World War II for example, the army of France's exiled government which fled to England and the American forces stationed in England were not occupying forces. In this situation, it was necessary for both France and the U.S. to come to an agreement with England about the status of their respective armed forces within that country. Thus, a conflict of sovereignties ensued, and the resulting agreement detailing the adjustment and suppression of U.S. and Allied sovereignty became what is known as a "Status of Forces Agreement." By nature of the agreement, it is impossible for either country to fully exercise its sovereignty. This is the fundamental result of a Status of Forces Agreement.

The North Atlantic Treaty Organization (NATO) forces stationed in Europe following World War II, U.S. armed forces stationed in Japan under the U.S.-Japan Security Treaty, and U.S. forces stationed in South Korea under the U.S.-Republic of Korea [South Korea] Mutual Defense Treaty are not occupying forces. Therefore, in concluding respective Status of Forces Agreements, the U.S. and the recipient countries mutually suppress their sovereignty. The issue, however, is whether the lines of demarcation of sovereignty are appropriate or not. For example, the long-standing presence of U.S. forces in Japan and South Korea closely resembles that of an occupying force. Because there is a perception that the line of demarcation treats the American forces as an occupying army and favors the U.S., Japan and South Korea are seeking to revise their Status of Forces Agreements.

If the current line of demarcation is deemed inappropriate, there are two ways to amend it. The first is to alter the agreement itself. The other method is to keep the provisions of the agreement as is, but to have both governments agree to improve its application. The latter is essentially a revision in practice and is the option that the governments of Japan and the U.S. have decided to pursue. They recognized that a formal revision would be costly in political terms, but those seeking a revision of the SOFA believe that simply altering the way the agreement is administered will be too weak.

There are at least two points of view concerning the revision of the SOFA. One revisionist argument repudiates the U.S.-Japan Security Treaty and ultimately demands the withdrawal of American forces, while the other argument approves of the treaty itself. In practical terms, it is hard to differentiate between these two arguments.

To explain why this is so, we must examine discussions in Japan concerning the U.S.-Japan Security Treaty since the Cold War. At that time, the ruling Liberal Democratic Party (LDP) promoted adherence to the Security Treaty while the opposition parties, led by the Japan Socialist Party (JSP), opposed it. With the end of the Cold War, the collapse of the 1955 System, and the growing tension surrounding North Korea, this structure disintegrated. The JSP lost political strength and the opposition forces that appeared in its place, led by the current Democratic Party of Japan (DPJ), no longer opposed the Security Treaty. To do so would harm relations with the U.S. and raise doubts concerning their ability to run the government.

Instead, an objective that is uniting the opposition forces is revision of the SOFA, with the main issues being criminal jurisdiction procedures and environmental problems. The former was highlighted by the 1995 rape and has aroused the emotions of the Japanese people. The latter, not foreseen in 1960 when the current SOFA was signed, provides further justification for a revision. Not only the opposition parties but also the ruling party find it difficult to oppose these issues. In addition, revision of the SOFA is not in opposition to the U.S.-Japan Security Treaty — on the contrary, it presumes the existence of the treaty — and therefore it does not meet resistance from ruling party politicians.

For example, a group of non-partisan members of Japan's National Diet known as the "Committee for the Revision of the SOFA and the Establishment of a True U.S.-Japan Partnership" has been formed to seek revision of the SOFA. In addition to former Vice-Minister for Foreign Affairs Toshio Kojima, who is serving as chairman, over one hundred members of both houses are participating, including former Minister of State for Defense Shigeru Ishiba, who serves as a consultant; Taro Kono, a member of the House of Representatives; and Masajuro Shiokawa, former Minister of Finance.

The committee's SOFA plan is a complete revision and consists of thirty-one articles, compared with the current SOFA's twenty-eight. The following are summaries of some of the articles:

■ ARTICLE 3.
Provision of Facilities and Areas:
The U.S. will be required to submit a plan for the intended use of bases every ten years.

■ ARTICLE 4.
Management of Facilities and External and Internal Areas:
Japanese authorities may enter bases after submitting an official notice in advance to base authorities or, in the event of an emergency, after simply making an announcement.

■ ARTICLE 7.
Principles Concerning Training:
Environmental impact studies on the effects of drills and training exercises will be conducted jointly by the U.S. and Japan every three years.

■ ARTICLE 12.
Driver's Licenses and Vehicles:
Only U.S. military personnel, civilian personnel employed by the U.S. military, and their dependents who carry both a driver's license and a certificate showing that they have received instruction on Japanese driving regulations will be permitted to drive off base.

■ ARTICLE 18.
Criminal Jurisdiction:
When Japan has primary jurisdiction, suspects will be held in a joint U.S.-Japan detention facility established by Japan until an indictment is issued. Following an indictment, Japan will take full custody of the suspect but will consider any U.S. request to keep the suspect in the joint detention facility.

■ ARTICLE 19.
Release of Claim:
Japanese victims of incidents or accidents caused by U.S. military personnel, off-duty civilian personnel employed by the U.S. military, or their dependents may receive the amount of compensation decided in court by the Japanese government.

■ ARTICLE 26.
Joint Investigative Council on Accidents:
A joint U.S.-Japan Investigative Council will be established and will investigate accidents in Japan resulting from American aircraft or ships in training or in transit.

This draft includes considerations from a number of angles, but the Japanese government has no plans to present these demands to the U.S. The government believes that improvement in the administration of the SOFA is already achieving favorable outcomes regarding both criminal jurisdiction and environmental problems. Where criminal jurisdiction is concerned, arrangements in line with those of NATO are already incorporated in the U.S.-Japan SOFA. Strict standards have been applied to environmental issues, and the Japanese right of entry into American bases is fundamentally recognized.

The U.S. has expressed its dissatisfaction over the issue of criminal jurisdiction in terms of protecting the human rights of American soldiers. It refused to hand over an American soldier to Japanese authorities prior to indictment during an attempted rape case in December 2002 known as "the Brown Incident," where the victim later retracted assertions made previously during the investigation and raised the possibility of the defendant's innocence.

The U.S. has been critical of Japanese investigative methods which tend to place emphasis on obtaining confessions from suspects and has demanded that a U.S. official be present during the questioning of all U.S. military personnel. After South Korea granted a similar request when the same problem occurred between the U.S. and South Korea, Japan and the U.S. in April 2004 reached an agreement on operational improvement in which Japan accepted this U.S. demand. That this issue was raised by the U.S. highlights the complexity of the SOFA problem in adjusting the sovereignty of both countries.

In Japan, the SOFA is regarded as a treaty and therefore a revision cannot be implemented without Diet approval. On the other hand, the U.S. regards the SOFA as an administrative agreement and therefore it can be amended within the authority of the U.S. Defense Department. Consideration of this aspect alone gives the impression that there are fewer impediments in the U.S. than in Japan.

In reality, however, there are impediments on both sides. First, the current SOFA consists of delicate adjustments of the sovereignty of two countries and any revision would involve many complex legal problems. Second, the U.S. is concerned that changing Japan's SOFA will negatively affect its SOFA agreements with South Korea and NATO. Third, there is recognition by authorities in both governments that the revision debate is largely based on emotional arguments and there is a strong view that the problems can be solved by improving the administration of the current agreement.

Therefore, before SOFA revision becomes a reality, Japan and particularly the U.S. would likely state that one of the following two cases needs to happen. First, regardless of whether or not the impetus for revision is emotional, an overwhelming demand for SOFA revision within Japan will cause both governments to realize the cost of maintaining the U.S.-Japan Security Alliance. In this case, for Japan as the weaker party to act in a threatening way would result in an unfortunate situation. Before this happens, both governments would probably make further attempts to improve administration of the SOFA and try to avoid a revision. Such a course might be acceptable to the public as long as there are concrete reductions in the number and scale of U.S. bases in Okinawa.

The second case entails SOFA revision if there is a major qualitative change in the U.S.-Japan Security Alliance, a change that is already occurring. American journalist Richard Halloran has described the composition of U.S. security relationships with other countries in the aftermath of the war in Iraq of 2003 as "2-3-4-5 and the Other 3." The first "2" are Canada and Mexico, the countries which share borders with the U.S. The "3" are Japan, Britain, and Australia, the U.S.'s most trusted allies. The "4" are the group next in importance: Italy, Spain, Poland, and Singapore. The "5" are the countries that did not support the U.S. during the war in Iraq: Turkey, France, Germany, China, and Russia. The "other 3" are Israel, South Korea, and Taiwan, countries that have a special relationship with the U.S. What is important here is that Japan has been ranked as high as Britain and Australia. If we focus on this point alone, we may think that the U.S. will regard Japan's SOFA more highly than the NATO SOFA which centers on Germany.

A qualitative change in the U.S.-Japan Security Alliance might result in a revision of the U.S.-Japan Security Treaty, a revision that would aim for a more reciprocal relationship. A fundamental review of the treaty's existing framework would result from a strengthened alliance relationship, which would come with continued initiatives like the enactment of a permanent law for international contribution that would make possible the engagement of Self-Defense Forces in overseas rear support activities; changes in the interpretation of the Constitution or an amendment to the Constitution concerning the exercise of the right of collective self-defense; and the strengthening of U.S.-Japan cooperation in missile defense.

While the SOFA revision draft by the non-partisan group of Diet members is well thought out, it lacks this overall perspective of the U.S.-Japan Security Alliance and focuses on the wording of the provisions. As long as the proposal remains narrow in its focus, there is little possibility that it will be considered by both governments; unless the other party can be satisfied, negotiations will not succeed. SOFA revision resulting from a strengthened U.S.-Japan Security Alliance is, however, probably beyond the scope of consideration for Okinawans, and it may not be the direction that they wish to choose. If this is the case, it is important that visible strides be made in consolidating bases in Okinawa.

Futenma as a Symbol of the U.S. Base Issue in Okinawa

The SACO Final Report gives the impression that the highly symbolic transfer of Futenma Air Station is lagging, because it was not accomplished within the proposed five to seven year period. In reality, however, apart from the return of Gimbaru Training Area, which is behind schedule due to adjustment matters between Futenma and the town of Kin, the measures in the Final Report are progressing satisfactorily. Specific procedures have already been decided for the return of facilities such as Sobe Communication Site, known as "the elephant's cage," and Yomitan Auxiliary Airfield in 2004.

The contents of the SACO agreement are not, however, limited to the return of land and facilities. They also include the improvement in training methods and administration of the SOFA mentioned previously. Live ammunition drills over Highway 104 have already ceased and have been reassigned to Self-Defense Force training grounds on the main Japanese islands. Parachute training at Yomitan Auxiliary Airfield, which had been a major problem, has been relocated to Ie Jima Auxiliary Airfield. To improve administration of the SOFA, several agreements have been reached including a joint statement on environmental principles.

The basic plan for the relocation of Futenma Air Station was decided at a Cabinet meeting on July 29, 2002. The plan is to build a facility offshore from the district of Henoko in the city of Nago. Currently, an environmental impact assessment is being conducted and is estimated to last until 2007. There have been numerous complications leading up to the relocation of Futenma. The following is a list of important developments:

- **December 21, 1997** — The majority of Nago residents oppose base relocation in a public referendum.
- **December 25, 1997** — Nago Mayor Tetsuya Higa announces the acceptance of the base and his resignation.
- **February 6, 1998** — Okinawa Governor Masahide Ota rejects the offshore facility proposal.
- **February 8, 1998** — Tateo Kishimoto, a member of the faction supporting acceptance of the base, wins the Nago mayoral election.
- **November 1998** — Keiichi Inamine, with the recommendation of the LDP, wins Okinawa's gubernatorial election.

The election of Keiichi Inamine as governor reinvigorated the relocation movement, but a campaign pledge he made has raised new problems. Inamine had stated that the establishment of a fifteen-year limit for the use of facilities by the American military was necessary in view of the Okinawan citizens' desire for base reduction and consolidation. However, the U.S. and Japan have not been about to agree on setting this limit in advance to fifteen years.

While the Japanese government recognizes that the time limit issue is difficult given the state of world affairs, it is seriously considering the requests of the governor of Okinawa and the mayor of Nago and will continue to discuss this issue, as well as the composition of U.S. military forces in Okinawa, with the U.S. government. However, when the Japanese government raises the time limit issue during discussions including U.S.-Japan summit meetings, the reaction of the U.S. has been negative. The international situation fifteen years from now is impossible to predict and in that respect the American view is understandable. The only realistic approach, therefore, is to consider the fifteen-year issue within a broad context involving the U.S. military forces in Okinawa and the entire framework of the U.S.-Japan Security Treaty.

The same is true for a solution to the SOFA revision debate. A realistic approach does not make the fifteen-year limit a precondition for the relocation of Futenma, but attempts to bring about a solution in the course of overall changes. In other words, the fifteen-year limit should not be a condition of the solution, but an outcome of it. In this volume, Kazuhisa Ogawa and Akikazu Hashimoto have made specific recommendations in this regard and details can be found in their chapters.

The Paradoxical Truth that a Stronger U.S.-Japan Security Alliance Will Lead to a Reduction in the Burden of the Bases

From Okinawa's point of view, the important issue is reducing the current burden of the bases, and implementation of the SACO's recommendations and SOFA revision are initiatives aimed at achieving this. Since both governments are adopting procedures for a material revision of the SOFA by improving its administration, discussions on SOFA revision have become emotional. The same can be said of the fifteen-year issue which has become the focus of SACO implementation. From a broader perspective, the best way to reduce the burden of the bases is to make the U.S.-Japan Security Alliance more reciprocal.

First, we must recognize the right of collective self-defense either through reinterpretation of or an amendment to the Constitution. The government is currently examining a permanent law whereby Japan could provide rear support for a country like the U.S. in the event of an international conflict. But without a reinterpretation or change in the Constitution, we cannot avoid highly legalistic and quasi-theological disputes about such issues as what constitutes a combat and non-combat zone. If Self-Defense Force personnel are dispatched to areas where there are disputes, consideration of their safety is only natural and there should be no problem in making individual policy decisions that provide for the particular circumstances of each situation. Legally-mandated deployment constraints obstruct effective, flexible movement and expose Self-Defense Force personnel to danger.

Secondly, the strengthening of the alliance that results from the exercise of collective self-defense mentioned above is also important. Reducing the burden of the bases in Okinawa and the right to collective self-defense may at a glance seem unrelated. However, consider Article 17 of SOFA that established criminal jurisdiction. The present U.S.-Japan SOFA has the same content as the NATO SOFA. If the NATO agreement that was concluded with the right to collective self-defense and the U.S.-Japan agreement that was concluded without it were the same in content, Japan's recognition of the right to collective self-defense would serve to strengthen the bilateral alliance. This factor would serve as a playing card that Japan could use to its advantage when it makes a request to the U.S. for a revision of the agreement.

The alliance relationship will not be strengthened through documents alone. Of utmost importance is onsite cooperation; one key cooperative aspect is missile defense. The use of the revolution in military affairs (RMA), including missile defense, has the potential to change the strategic meaning of U.S. military power in Okinawa. That, in itself, holds possibilities in regard to bringing about a reduction in the military forces in Okinawa. If force reduction in Okinawa is caused by the RMA, this outcome will not send any strategic messages that could be misunderstood in Japan or the rest of the world.

Third, the divisions among the four branches of the U.S. armed forces (Army, Navy, Air Force, and Marine Corps) must be overcome. Concerning the relocation of the Marine Corps' Futenma Air Station, the Air Force supposedly rejected the proposal to relocate Futenma to its Kadena Air Base. Obstructions like these can occur in any bureaucratic organization and leaders must overcome them. In this context, if those top leaders need a compelling reason to convince their organizations, it would be the realization of a stronger U.S.-Japan Security Alliance.

If the majority of Okinawans are opposed to the U.S.-Japan security framework, the strengthening of the alliance as a means of reducing the burden of the bases would probably appear as a contradiction in their eyes. The security alliance is, so to speak, a national consensus and there is little likelihood of a political party attempting to dissolve it at this time. Therefore, if the burden of the bases is reduced in a visible way, it may bring about a change in those who are speaking out in Okinawa. For this reason, it is necessary for the Japanese government to continue to focus on Okinawa.

Aerial view of the U.S. Marine Corps' Futenma Air Station, Ginowan, Okinawa. (Okinawa Prefectural Government, Military Base Affairs Office)

A Grand Bargain for a Sustainable U.S. Military Presence in Okinawa

Kazuhisa Ogawa
Military Analyst

How can Japan resolve the problems arising from the presence of U.S. military bases in Okinawa, and give its citizens viable options for the future of their society and economy? Any such initiative must simultaneously satisfy three conditions: (1) return some of the bases and reduce and consolidate the others; (2) advance initiatives that will wean Okinawa's economy from its dependency on the bases and Japanese national government handouts; and (3) maintain a U.S. military presence.

Japan must, therefore, achieve the return, consolidation, and reduction of U.S. bases in Okinawa while using the remaining bases to the best possible advantage for its economic development. In this paper, I discuss several indispensable steps, including the relocation of U.S. bases within Okinawa. Some of my plans are likely to provoke fierce opposition from the Okinawan citizens. Nevertheless, I present this radical view knowing it will invite criticism, because I believe Okinawa needs a strong suit of cards to emerge a winner from negotiations with the United States.

Step 1: Relocate Futenma Air Station to Camp Hansen

The bilateral agreement for the return of the U.S. Marine Corps' Futenma Air Station to Japan is a viable beachhead for resolving the issue of U.S. bases in Okinawa and designing a groundbreaking economic development plan for the islands. A realistic way forward consists of two steps, to be implemented at the same time if possible.

Before presenting Step 1, I will present a brief history of the Futenma Air Station relocation issue since the Special Action Committee on Okinawa (SACO) Interim Report of April 15, 1996, which first stipulated the return of Futenma. As of July 2003, relocation is still deadlocked.

In December 1997, the majority rejected a referendum in the city of Nago proposing the construction of an offshore helicopter base as stated in the SACO Final Report on Futenma Air Station of December 2, 1996 (See Appendix). Nevertheless, Nago Mayor Tetsuya Higa expressed his intention to accept the proposal and then tendered his resignation. Okinawa Governor Masahide Ota refused to accept the plan, but former Nago Deputy Mayor Tateo Kishimoto was elected mayor of Nago with the support of former mayors and in 1999 consented to the proposal. (Kishimoto was reelected in 2002.) Okinawa Governor Keiichi Inamine, who defeated the incumbent in the election of November 1998, formally declared in November 1999 that Futenma will relocate to "the coastal area of Henoko in Nago within the waters of the U.S. Marine Corps' Camp Schwab," subject to conditions like the fifteen-year limit on usage.

The national and local government authorities discussed this issue in the Facility Relocation Council. In June 2001, the Council presented a total of eight plans using three different construction methods: (1) the quick installation pier (QIP), which is supported by stakes; (2) the pontoon method, in which a box-shaped steel structure is floated at sea; and (3) land reclamation.

On July 29, 2002, the Facility Relocation Council agreed on a basic plan to build a helicopter base with a total length of 2,500 meters by reclaiming land over a coral reef off the district of Henoko in Nago. Although the Council decided to commence a pre-works environmental impact assessment, it postponed decision on the fifteen-year limit on military usage sought by the Okinawan government.

Having reviewed the history, as Step 1, I propose relocating Futenma to a new facility on existing land within Okinawa, such as the Marine Corps' Camp Hansen. Futenma currently occupies 481.5 hectares and its runway is 2,800 meters long, the same as Fukuoka Airport. It is home to 12 KC-130 in-flight refueling aircraft and helicopter squadrons of Marine Aircraft Group 36's 1st Marine Aircraft Wing. Camp Hansen occupies 5,147.1 hectares and is 10.7 times the area of Futenma. Relocation of Futenma's runway and other facilities would call for consolidating all of Camp Hansen's existing facilities, including barracks, within its grounds.

This option may invite opposition from the Okinawan citizens, because relocation would take place within the prefecture. I firmly believe, however, that this option is worth investigating; it offers a powerful card for persuading the United States to return, consolidate, and reduce its bases within Okinawa; reduce the Marine Corps' footprint (described later as "Ready Rear-Area Deployment"); and convert the U.S. Air Force's Kadena Air Base into a multiuse hub airport.

Just how effective a trump card would it be in solving the various problems facing Okinawa? Until the SACO Interim Report was issued on April 15, 1996, the United States had refused to return Futenma, saying that while relocation of Futenma's forces to Kadena Air Base and the Marine Corps' Iwakuni Air Station was feasible under normal situations, it was unworkable during emergencies. The argument was based on the number of aircraft that would come from the U.S. mainland to render assistance in case of an emergency — approximately 200 Air Force aircraft to Kadena and approximately 300 Marine Corps aircraft to Futenma.

Even from the perspective of maintaining a military presence, the U.S. assertion does have certain validity. The III Marine Expeditionary Force (III MEF) headquartered in Okinawa has only 19,265 personnel and approximately 100 aircraft deployed in Japan as of July 2003, but there is no guarantee that the fully complemented I MEF (44,496 personnel and 456 aircraft) and II MEF (45,674 personnel and 367 aircraft) will not be deployed. Moreover, although the III MEF has fewer troops than the other MEFs in peacetime, it has the same quota of equipment like tanks, artillery, and aircraft as the I MEF, and its troop strength could mushroom to the levels of other MEFs.

Specifically, a fully complemented Marine air wing like the I MEF's 3rd Marine Aircraft Wing is equipped with a total of 456 aircraft, both fixed-wing aircraft (64 AV-8B V/STOL strike aircraft, 84 F/A-18 strike fighters, and 12 KC-130 in-flight refueling aircraft) and helicopters (90 CH-46 transport helicopters, 64 CH-53 transport helicopters, 50 UH-1N utility helicopters, and 92 AH-1 attack helicopters). Occasionally, EA-6B electronic warfare aircraft join them.

Even in the case of an emergency like the one described by U.S. opponents of returning Futenma to Japan, if a replacement air facility on the same scale as Futenma were built in Camp Hansen, the Air Force would be able to operate many C-5A/B Galaxy aircraft to supply the Marine air wing. (This giant transport aircraft can fly 5,522 kilometers loaded with a maximum payload of 118 tons. It can take off fully loaded within 2,530 meters.) Moreover, even if a fully complemented MEF were deployed in Okinawa, the replacement air facility would be able to accommodate most of its aircraft and supplies. The proposed Henoko offshore helicopter base, with its 1,500 meter-long runway, could not fulfill these functions. This base was designed with the operation of only the V-22 Osprey V/STOL utility aircraft in mind. (The V-22's maximum cruising speed is 582 kilometers per hour; its range is 2,224 kilometers; and it can carry twenty-eight crew and troops.)

With such a serious proposal, there would be a greater likelihood of reducing the peacetime troop strength of Marine ground units in Okinawa, if the Japanese side negotiated with some skill. Okinawan citizens resent the Marine presence in Camp Hansen and Camp Schwab and my plan is for these troops to deploy and train in peacetime in a U.S. territory like Hawai'i, or in third countries like Australia or the Philippines. Unlike in past proposals for "emergency deployment," this rear-area deployment with a high level of readiness (which I will call "Ready Rear-Area Deployment") will be designed around an agreement regarding emergencies in which troops would return to Okinawa rapidly when signs of international military tension appear, e.g., within twenty-four hours.

This Ready Rear-Area Deployment would utilize the strategic mobility of the Civil Reserve Air Fleet (CRAF), the effectiveness of which was demonstrated during the Persian Gulf War of 1991. In mid-August 1990, shortly after the Iraqi invasion of Kuwait, the I MEF completed deployment from California to Saudi Arabia in 2.5 days, and the 4th Marine Expeditionary Brigade did so in 6 days from the East Coast. The core of that strategic mobility was the CRAF, which airlifted 75,000 troops and 65,000 tons of materiel to the theater in just one month. In particular, in the first few weeks of the war, CRAF and other aircraft arrived in Saudi Arabia at the rate of one every ten minutes.

What would Ready Rear-Area Deployment require in terms of the U.S. military footprint in Okinawa? Camp Hansen and Camp Schwab must be maintained to receive ground troops. Security personnel (and their families) must remain in Okinawa to maintain base functions for the Maritime Prepositioning Ships (MPS) deployed in the Indian Ocean and near the Mariana Islands. The United States deploys three MPS squadrons: MPS Squadron One (five ships in the Mediterranean), MPS Squadron Two (six ships near Diego Garcia), and MPS Squadron Three (five ships near the Mariana Islands). Each MPS squadron carries equipment and thirty days of supplies for one Marine expeditionary brigade (16,500–17,600 troops).

Relocation of Futenma Air Station to Camp Hansen would enable the Marine Corps to keep its air power in Okinawa while putting on Ready Rear-Area Deployment most of the Marines who are currently deployed on the island. There should be no reason why the U.S. would not engage in negotiations on the return or consolidation and reduction of U.S. bases and the Ready Rear-Area Deployment of Marines. Although there are some technical issues like overcoming Camp Hansen's topographic problems, noise problems and operational risks could be largely controlled through careful design of the runway and flight paths. In addition, this option avoids the waste of constructing an offshore helicopter base and the destruction of the maritime environment that would result.

There will be no prospect of resolving these problems, be they noise pollution or the risk of accidents, without ideas and processes that minimize their occurrence. Environmental problems occur not just in the construction of new bases but also in the building of hospitals and churches. Therefore, this topic requires some compromise. It should be borne in mind, however, that Okinawa's most precious natural environment is the sea.

The importance of Okinawa's maritime environment, however, does not mean just anywhere on land is suitable for Futenma Air Station's replacement facility. Under no circumstance should Futenma be integrated into Kadena Air Base. This option which eliminates the need to construct another base may ease the segment of the public opposed to new bases within the prefecture. This is why both the prefectural and national governments, who lacked the confidence to persuade citizens to accept relocation to a newly built facility within the prefecture, initially persisted with the Kadena integration proposal. This proposal, however, poses the danger of making the U.S. military presence in Kadena nearly permanent. In such a case, there would be no hope for plans like converting Kadena to a hub airport, which I will discuss next. Therefore, relocation of Futenma to Kadena may be suicidal for Okinawa's future.

Step 2: Civil-Military Airport in Camp Schwab, and Kadena as a Hub Airport

Step 2 involves building a civil-military airport in Camp Schwab (2077.6 hectares, 4.3 times the area of Futenma), as a part of a groundbreaking program for the economic development of Okinawa, and operating Kadena Air Base as Asia's hub airport in coordination with the civil-military airport.

Aircraft that must be stationed permanently in Okinawa like the F-15 fighters in Kadena would operate from this civil-military airport. Major units such as the wing headquarters, the air-refueling squadron, and the airborne air control squadron would relocate to the main Japanese islands, but an emergency agreement would be concluded so these units could return to Kadena rapidly, say within six hours, when sign of military conflict appears. Naturally, even if Kadena were operated as a hub airport, its military function would be maintained to ensure readiness in the event of an emergency; Air Force security personnel would also continue to be stationed there.

These arrangements would meet U.S. concerns about reduction in military presence, and would prevent neighboring countries from misperceiving that the U.S. military is leaving Japan. Also, in a military emergency, rerouting most of Kadena's civilian air traffic to other airports like the civil-military airport in Camp Schwab should not be a problem, because civilian air traffic would be minimal in such a circumstance.

Chitose Air Base located in Hokkaido offers the best conditions for relocating the Air Force's major units from Kadena. Only the 2nd Air Wing of Japan's Air Self-Defense Force has used Chitose Air Base since the New Chitose Airport opened. The space for civilian aircraft, where wide-body aircraft used to land, could be used again with a few upgrades. Once the prospects for controlling noise pollution and the risk of accidents are in hand, the Hokkaido government may well accept major units from Kadena. Then, the units that move to Chitose Air Base would be able to share training airspace with the U.S. Air Force's 35th Fighter Wing at Misawa Air Base in Aomori Prefecture. As a result, Okinawa's training airspace would become less crowded and air traffic control would improve.

The civil-military airport at Camp Schwab would pay dividends not just for the northern region but for the development of Okinawa as a whole, if it were utilized as a servicing base for civil aviation in all of Asia, as the Okinawa Prefectural Government and I have proposed. If the Japanese and Okinawan governments have the business acumen, they could negotiate with Boeing or Airbus to establish a facility for high-level maintenance of passenger aircraft within the civil-military airport, an undertaking unique in the Asia-Pacific region. In that event, Okinawa can expect to attract aerospace and related industries on a large scale, as well as colleges and universities, which would mean jobs and population growth.

In this scenario, two 4,000-meter runways would be desirable for the civil-military airport. The local population would no doubt greet this proposal with more understanding than with an airbase for military purposes. Noise pollution presents the biggest concern, but Shimoji Island, which has a 3,000-meter runway for civilian air training, may accept post-servicing test flights and thus mitigate some of the increased noise.

The Self-Defense Forces' air units (the Ground SDF, 101th Squadron; the Maritime SDF, Fleet Air Wing 5; and the Air SDF, Southwestern Composite Air Division) are currently sharing Naha Airport and its one 3,000-meter runway. This airport could be dismantled and the land could be redeveloped as an economic center oriented toward the rest of Asia. In that event, all Self-Defense Force aircraft would be transferred from Naha Airport to the civil-military airport at Camp Schwab. Most civilian flights would use the Kadena hub airport, and the rest would use the civil-military airport.

On a related note, why are Marine Corps bases concentrated in Okinawa? Unlike with Army, Navy, and Air Force bases, the United

States prefers to concentrate Marine Corps bases in Okinawa instead of dispersing them throughout the Japanese islands. U.S. officials cite Okinawa's location in relation to third countries and the technical desirability of collocating bases and training grounds, but these reasons do not tell the whole story. Remembering its sacrifice in the Battle of Okinawa of World War II, the Marine Corps may view Okinawa as its prize for victory in that battle, but this still does not account for the concentration of its bases on the island.

Ever since the end of World War II, the Marine Corps in Okinawa has not only guarded against the Soviet Union and China, but also against the potential military revival of Japan. The iron law of crisis management is to prepare for the worst. The Marine Corps has remained vigilant to ensure that Japan remains a U.S. ally and to secure in Okinawa some of Japan's functions as a power projection platform, even if the U.S.-Japan Security Alliance was to break down. This issue, however, will not come to light as long as the alliance continues. For this reason, relocation within the prefecture is essential for resolving the issue of Marine Corps bases in Okinawa like Futenma Air Station.

Take Economic Advantage of Okinawa's Location with a Hub Airport

I have portrayed the above initiative with the relocation of Futenma Air Station as the beachhead, because there are two prerequisites for viewing Okinawa's future as one of limitless potential. First, Okinawa needs an airport and a seaport that can take advantage of its location 1,500 km from both Tokyo and Manila, and serve as the hub of Asia. Second, based on the history of warfare on the island, Okinawa should develop as a world-class center for the research and practice of peace.

If these prerequisites can be met, then the success of schemes for a free trade zone and an "international city," where capital and industries from around the world would converge, would be assured. Conversely, an expedient compromise would truncate their growth potential, and would risk keeping Okinawa dependent on colonial-style handouts through much of the twenty-first century.

Of the two prerequisites, the provision of a hub airport in particular would have a decisive impact on Okinawa's future. When deciding where to locate a world-class hub airport in Okinawa, it is difficult to avoid considering Kadena Air Base, for nearly 100 aircraft, such as the F-15 fighters of the Air Force's 18th Wing, are deployed there regularly. On one hand, the United States is not likely to ever return Kadena as long as the U.S.-Japan Security Treaty remains in force. On the other, Kadena will continue to stunt Okinawa's development as long as it remains a base dedicated to military use in the island's densely populated heartland. This dilemma leaves one desirable course: convert Kadena into a hub airport at least for peacetime use, and make it the focus of Okinawa's development.

Kadena Air Base now covers 2,043 hectares, and has two runways of 3,650 meters each. It is comparable to the new airports springing up around Asia, and has enough space for two more runways. In all of Japan, there is hardly any other location where land could be acquired on a scale comparable to the new Asian airports.

The Japanese and U.S. governments have decided to relocate Naha Port to the city of Urasoe. A large civilian port facility should be built in Urasoe alongside the military port. An important element in boosting Okinawa's economy is to make this port a world-class hub port in conjunction with the conversion of Kadena to a hub airport. The scheme for a free trade zone in Okinawa would be viable only with both a hub airport and a hub seaport.

The Two Nations' Stakes in Reducing the U.S. Military Footprint in Okinawa

Seventy-five percent of the total land used exclusively by the U.S. military in Japan is concentrated within Okinawa. In theory, there are three ways to lift this burden.

First, Japan may terminate the U.S.-Japan Security Treaty. In that event, in accordance with Article 10 of the treaty, U.S. forces would withdraw from Japan within a year, and U.S. bases would also presumably cease to exist. For several decades, Japanese supporters of the treaty have assumed that if Japan angered the United States, then the U.S. would revoke the security treaty and leave Japan's security seriously exposed. Without the security treaty with Japan, however, the United States would no longer be able to use Japan as its power projection platform. Then, the United States would be likely to lose its global leadership position. Clearly, the United States has more to lose from termination of the security treaty with Japan. In terms of strategic dependence on the alliance, it is no exaggeration to say that the United States has feared termination of the treaty by Japan.

If Japan sought termination, then U.S. bases would disappear from Okinawa and elsewhere in Japan. Moreover, if Japan were to take a hard line and show the resolve to put the alliance with the United States on the table, then it should be possible to extract major concessions from the U.S. toward the resolution of the issue of U.S. bases in Okinawa.

The second option is for Okinawa to secede from Japan unilaterally. The instant Okinawa declares independence, it would fall outside the framework of the U.S.-Japan Security Treaty. Unless Japan intervenes militarily, the U.S. bases in Okinawa could be removed about a year later. If the United States then wished to keep its bases in Okinawa, Okinawa would be able to represent its interests directly to the U.S. without the frustration of negotiating through Tokyo. Okinawa could expect massive economic assistance in this scenario, even if independence brings certain risks and even if many U.S. bases remain. Okinawa could then conceivably build up the infrastructure for supporting itself as a trading state on a par with Singapore.

Nevertheless, both the termination of the U.S.-Japan Security Treaty and the secession of Okinawa would seriously undermine Japan's national interests. Consider the termination of the security treaty. Asian countries trust Japan to the extent they do because Japan is allied to the United States. Should Japan revoke the security treaty, thereby throwing off U.S. restraints, the Asian countries would be more wary of Japanese behavior, especially those of a military nature, for Japan has not settled issues remaining from World War II to their satisfaction. Also, withdrawal of the U.S. military from Japan may trigger an arms race among Asian countries that are uneasy about China's military behavior. Then, those countries would blame Japan for triggering this arms race, and trust Japan even less.

Secession of Okinawa would be another nightmare scenario for Japan. Secession would likely weaken Japan's international influence due to its perceived inability to resolve a relatively straightforward domestic problem like the U.S. base issue. Moreover, loss of Okinawa may well halve Japan's value as a U.S. power projection platform, and thereby weaken Japan's bargaining leverage with the United States.

All the parties involved especially Okinawan citizens must realize, however, that neither option has ever gained the support of the majority either in Okinawa or in Japan as a whole. The majority of both populations have concluded that the attendant risks are too great. Prudent Japanese and U.S. citizens should not need any evidence beyond these Japanese national interests, which are also U.S. national interests, to understand the need to lighten the burden on Okinawan citizens by consolidating U.S. bases or relocating them to the main Japanese islands.

Pacification of the U.S.-Japan Security Alliance

Hence, a third option becomes more realistic: pacification of the U.S.-Japan Security Alliance. By this, I mean a comprehensive process for realizing international peace that includes (1) operation of the alliance according to Japan's fundamental principles of peaceful settlement of international disputes and support for the United Nations' role in international peace and security, (2) promotion of worldwide disarmament, (3) qualitative evolution of the alliance, and (4) return and consolidation of U.S. bases in Japan. Although I do not doubt the sincerity of the Japanese opponents of U.S. bases in the post-World War II era, their slogans and political actions, by themselves, have failed to resolve the issue in a desirable way. This historical reality demonstrates the importance of pacifying the U.S.-Japan Security Alliance.

In this context, one way to make the U.S.-Japan Security Alliance more consistent with Japan's aforementioned principles is to give U.S. bases in Okinawa a role as a power projection platform for worldwide peacekeeping through the United Nations. Three U.S. bases in Okinawa — Kadena, Futenma, and the Navy's White Beach Area — have been designated as United Nations bases since the Korean War. Japan and the United States should make them major bases of U.N. peacekeeping operations, and establish peacekeeping training centers and posts for a U.N. standby force similar to that of the Nordic countries. (Futenma would relocate with its role in the United Nations.) Japan's financial support and territorial defense of these bases for peacekeeping operations should be acknowledged explicitly as part of Japanese burden sharing in the U.S.-Japan Security Alliance, not just as its contribution to the United Nations. In that event, Japan would need to confirm through bilateral consultation that U.S. bases in Japan are being used by U.S. forces that participate in U.N. peacekeeping operations.

For third countries, this option confirms that the United States will keep bases in Japan as its power projection platform, and therefore Japan will act militarily only in concert with the United States. The latter point is a significant merit of this option; it eases Asian nations' concerns about Japanese military behavior.

Conclusion

The process outlined above, including relocation of U.S. bases within Okinawa, is also one of realistic management toward the best possible outcome. Sometimes, we must take otherwise undesirable paths to resolve larger problems.

In any event, alliances are about national interests. Japan should manage its alliance with the United States to suit its national interests by operating it in accordance with Japan's principles, thereby contributing to world peace and, in doing so, winning trust and security. Otherwise, Japan cannot claim to be a peace-loving country without inviting derision.

Recall this proposal's basic approach: the aim is fundamental resolution of the problems arising from the U.S. military presence in Okinawa. Therefore, we should not think small about Okinawa's socioeconomic development, in a rush to settle on the relocation site for Futenma Air Station. A drastic return of U.S. bases in Okinawa, like that which occurred in the Philippines with the closing of bases like the Air Force's Clark Air Base and the Navy's Subic Naval Base on December 31, 1992, is inconceivable because Japan constitutes a power projection platform without which the United States cannot exercise global leadership.

In that sense, the return of Futenma Air Station, which was sought at the political level by former Prime Minister Ryutaro Hashimoto, may be described as a historic milestone in Japanese foreign policy. That achievement is one more reason that subsequent initiatives for Okinawa's development should not be trivialized.

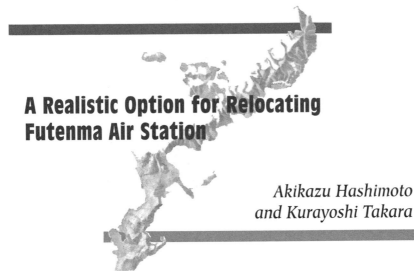

A Realistic Option for Relocating Futenma Air Station

Akikazu Hashimoto
and Kurayoshi Takara

T he relocation of the U.S. Marine Corps' Futenma Air Station has been the most challenging and vital aspect of the Special Action Committee on Okinawa (SACO) Final Report of December 2, 1996 (See Appendix). The original target date of seven years after the SACO report (i.e. 2003) for returning Futenma has already passed. The political and technical difficulties of the Japanese and American governments' plan to build a replacement facility on the coastal waters off the U.S. Marine Corps' Camp Schwab in the district of Henoko in the city of Nago have led some to advocate that this option be abandoned in favor of an alternative.

For example, there have been proposals calling for integrating many of the functions now served by Futenma into the U.S. Air Force's Kadena Air Base. Although supporters of this option stress that take-offs and landings should be limited to or reduced from current levels at Kadena after the integration takes place, we oppose this proposal because it would incite strong opposition from local residents living near Kadena. Moreover, this alternative would entrench Kadena as a quasi-permanent base, thereby restricting Kadena's future functions for the Okinawan people. The proposal to relocate some of Futenma functions to Shimoji Island Pilot Training Airfield would also be resisted by local residents.

In chapter VI of this volume, Kazuhisa Ogawa outlined his creative proposal of integrating the Futenma functions into the U.S. Marine Corps' Camp Hansen. This option has the merit of protecting Okinawa's waters, an irreplaceable resource, and making U.S. Marine Corps operations more efficient through consolidation. By avoiding an increase in U.S. military operations out of Kadena, it also leaves open the possibility of transforming Kadena in the future into a hub airport for Okinawa as a whole.

All things considered, we believe that the best possible and most realistic option would be a *variation* of the governments' plan to move ahead with constructing an offshore relocation facility in Henoko, as mandated by the SACO Final Report. In advocating this position, we emphasize the following two objectives:

1) reduce the excessive burden on the Okinawan people (through base reduction and consolidation, U.S. Marine Corps personnel reduction, and protection of the Okinawan people's safety and peace of mind) and

2) maintain and improve the efficiency of the Okinawan base functions to be able to accurately respond to emergencies in the Asia-Pacific region. But given the acute dangers that Futenma poses due to its location in a densely populated urban area, we propose that its functions be temporarily transferred to other locations as soon as possible.

Moving Ahead with Relocation to Henoko

One the major criticisms against the Henoko option is that completion of the new offshore facility might take fifteen to seventeen years. From the time the environmental impact assessment was initiated in 2003, therefore, the estimated year of completion would be between 2018 and 2020. But we feel that the construction process can and should be accelerated.

Building the new offshore Henoko facility entails the following necessary steps:

1) Perform an environmental impact assessment (including procedures to meet legal requirements),

2) Construct a temporary yard,

3) Fill in the yard to create a flat surface,

4) Build the airport facilities, and

5) Make the airport functional (by relocating material and equipment).

To reduce the construction time, steps 2 through 5 above should not be performed sequentially, but should be performed *simultaneously* to the extent possible. If done in this way, experts have calculated that construction would take seven to eight years (the American company Bechtel estimates seven years at the earliest and nine and a half years at the latest). In other words, seven to eight years after a start date in 2007 would result in completion in 2014–15, rather than 2018–2020.

But even with this accelerated schedule, there is still the danger of tragic accidents happening in Futenma's vicinity in the interim as demonstrated by the U.S. helicopter crash in August 2004. Such accidents would irreparably damage the public's willingness to continue to host

U.S. military facilities in Okinawa. We therefore propose that the risks inherent in Futenma should be reduced dramatically by dispersing the more dangerous base functions elsewhere. These high-risk functions of Futenma should be temporarily transferred, with a predetermined time limit on use, to one of the other bases in Okinawa such as Shimoji Island Pilot Training Airfield, Camp Hansen, Camp Schwab, and Kadena Air Base (helicopters could be transferred to the U.S.-owned golf course), or to a location outside the prefecture or even the country. Even if all of the base functions are temporarily shifted elsewhere, Futenma would remain in place until the Henoko relocation facility is completed and transfer of the base is finished.

Okinawa Governor Keiichi Inamine is demanding that the usage of the relocation facility be limited to fifteen years. If this demand results in a deadlock, then the following alternative proposal should be offered. After construction begins, a review should be made every five years (starting in 2012) on the status of the facility, including the purpose and time limit of its use, for the following ten years (2022). In other words, rather than an overly restrictive "time limit" *(kigen)*, we should be thinking of renewable "terms" *(kikan)* for use of the new Henoko facility. Such an arrangement would give Okinawan citizens a meaningful voice in discussions about the existence and operations of U.S. bases in Okinawa.

Charred remains of the CH-53D helicopter, which took off from the U.S. Marine Corps' Futenma Air Station and crashed on August 13, 2004, at the campus of Okinawa International University. (Okinawa Times)

Thinking beyond Henoko

We must also consider the possibility that the Henoko option might fail
the environmental impact assessment. Under this scenario, relocation
would have to start again from scratch and other options would have to
be considered, including transferring Futenma's functions to a location
outside Okinawa or even the country (e.g. Guam). More optimistically,
there is also the possibility that a dramatic restructuring of the U.S. Marine
Corps presence in Okinawa as a result of America's military transformation
might make Futenma or the Henoko relocation facility unnecessary. But
the best scenario for Okinawa would be an improvement in the security
situation in the Asia-Pacific region that would permit a dramatic reduction
in the U.S. Marine Corps presence in Okinawa. If this were to happen,
Okinawa could use its strategic location to contribute more to regional
economic prosperity and peace as part of an "East Asian Community."

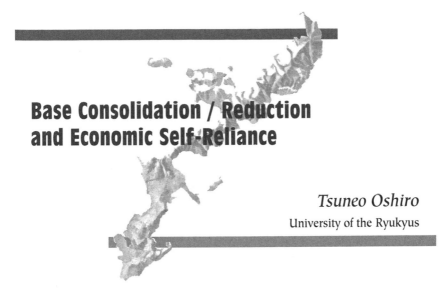

Base Consolidation / Reduction and Economic Self-Reliance

Tsuneo Oshiro
University of the Ryukyus

An Overview — Awareness of the Okinawa Question

O kinawa is a mystifying island and its population continues to grow. Since its reversion to Japan in 1972, the population has grown at twice the national rate, and in the past ten years, at three times the national rate. With an increase of 360,000 people since its reversion, Okinawa's population stands today at 1.33 million.

An increase in population can be an indicator of prosperity, where people are free to choose where they live and work, but Okinawa has the lowest per capita income, the highest unemployment rate, and the largest number of military bases in Japan. Yet its population continues to grow. University graduates in Okinawa hope to find employment within their prefecture and almost all of those who find jobs in the main Japanese islands return to Okinawa within several years.

Japanese people live longer than anyone else in the world, and Okinawans on average live longer than people in the rest of Japan. Thus, Okinawans live longer than people in any other place in the world. Okinawa also has the highest fertility rate in Japan, and is therefore the prefecture with the youngest population. It also has the highest divorce rate in Japan. This could be indicative of Okinawan society's compassion to accept without discrimination those who divorce, unlike the main Japanese islands, or perhaps the influence of American culture which has been in Okinawa for nearly sixty years.

Today, Okinawa is developing as a tourist hotspot and is the most popular Japanese destination for extended stays. In recent years, it has become highly regarded as a place for winter training camps for Japan's professional baseball and soccer teams as well as other athletes. It is reported that Okinawa is also the most preferred destination for American soldiers stationed overseas.

For Japanese in search of spiritual rather than material wealth, Okinawa may well be the place which reminds them of values they were beginning to forget: family, health, free time, space, and human relations. Okinawa is known for its lacquerware, pottery, dyed textiles, and shamisen music. It is also known for its unique lifestyle characterized by "Okinawan time," tege ("by and large" open-minded way of regarding life without worrying about unnecessary details), strong personal ties, yakuzen "healing herbal" cuisine, and adages like "once we meet, we become brothers and sisters forever."

Okinawan people can certainly be proud of their culture and history. The existence of a slow-paced lifestyle in tune with nature in the tropics may also be highly valued by those in a stressful society. At the same time, the tragic experience of war and the pain of being marginalized as a minority group are also experiences of the Okinawan people. There are many messages that Okinawa could share with all of us.

Okinawa is receiving increasing attention as a place for international conventions and projects. It has hosted the Kyushu-Okinawa Summit 2000 and the Pacific Island Leaders Meeting 2003 and will likely host a conference of the Inter-American Development Bank (IDB) in 2005. In addition, Okinawa attracts post-graduate projects from prestigious universities around the world.

The World Uchinanchu Business Association (WUB) whose mission is to increase cooperation among Uchinanchu ("Okinawan") business professionals around the world has continued to expand its network. In this way, along with attracting others to its island home, Okinawa is casting its sights outwards from Japan to the Asia-Pacific region and beyond.

In his "Cornerstone of Peace" speech, former U.S. President Bill Clinton stated,

> Okinawa has played an especially vital role in the endurance of our alliance. I know the people of Okinawa did not ask to play this role — hosting more than fifty percent of America's forces in Japan on less than one percent of Japan's land mass....we will continue to do what we can to reduce our footprint on this island. We take seriously our responsibility to be good neighbors....In the Information Age of the 21st century, Okinawa again can be a crossroads and a gateway between Japan and the rest of the world.[1]

Our objective is to head in the very direction suggested by President Clinton. Is Okinawa of value only as a military base? Is there not a way in which we can combine the hopes of the Okinawans, who seek peace, and the national interests of the United States and Japan? I would like to shed light on this issue and, in so doing, would like to shift the view of Okinawa from "a crossroads and a gateway between Japan and the rest of the world" to an "intelligent solution mechanism" linking Japan and the Asia-Pacific region.[2]

As one step in that direction, I will examine the U.S. military base issue and the possibility of Okinawa becoming a self-reliant economy. I will point out that the bases in Okinawa, constructed during the Cold War era, have magnified a contradiction regarding the economic development of Okinawa. I will then suggest a possible strategy for resolving this contradiction through the redefinition of Okinawa as soft power, which will also benefit both Japan and the U.S.

Why Is Reduction and Realignment of the Bases Necessary?

The existence of U.S. bases is said to be obstructing the robust develop–ment of Okinawa's economy and society. I would like to present four arguments in support of this thesis and the reduction and realignment of the bases.

(1) THE EXTENSIVE MILITARY BASES ARE SUBSTANTIALLY RESTRICTING LAND USE.

As Okinawa's population increases and economic activity expands, it is only natural that friction and tension increase between the U.S. bases and private sector areas. Land, which is a scarce resource in Okinawa, presents a tradeoff; where it is used by the bases it cannot be utilized by the private sector. Demanding the return of the bases to secure space and enable regional development is a logical course of action.

Current statistics help describe the heavy burden of U.S. military bases in Okinawa. Seventy-five percent (approximately twenty-four thousand hectares) of the total land used exclusively by the U.S. military in Japan is concentrated within Okinawa, which comprises only 0.6% of Japan's total land area.[3] Almost all of the bases in Okinawa Prefecture (ninety-six percent) are concentrated on the main island, where ninety-one percent of the prefecture's population (1.22 million people) lives and where approximately ninety percent of private businesses conduct their activities, and these bases occupy approximately twenty percent of the area of the main island.

Furthermore, the important bases are concentrated in the central region of the main island. Eighty-three percent of the land area of the town of Kadena is occupied by Kadena Air Base, the Far East's largest

U.S. Air Force base, and there is no land left for spatial development. The same is true for neighboring areas, where bases occupy fifty-six percent of the town of Chatan, forty-five percent of the village of Yomitan, thirty-six percent of the city of Okinawa, and thirty-three percent of the city of Ginowan. In this central area of the main island, the bases are spread in a mosaic pattern, greatly reducing the area available for development of the private sector economy and severely restricting municipalities in the development and maintenance of their economic and social foundations, including town planning, the development of road networks, and the establishment of a safe living environment.

In the main Japanese islands, eighty-nine percent of the land on which bases are located is nationally owned land while sixty-six percent of the land occupied by bases in Okinawa is owned by the prefecture, municipalities, or private individuals and families. This has been a factor complicating the base issue in Okinawa. Many of the bases were formed from land unilaterally expropriated from the prefecture, municipalities, and the private sector by the U.S. during its twenty-seven years of rule before reversion to Japan in 1972. In the central district where many of the important bases are located, seventy-six percent of the land the bases occupy is privately owned, with sixteen percent owned by the cities and towns, and only eight percent owned by the national government.

Because of the way that the bases developed, administrative districts and people's livelihoods and economic activities were cut off from each other by the bases, and city areas that subsequently developed under these complicated conditions suffered from a deteriorating environment, a decline in commercial functions, and decreased vitality. In addition, the bases brought noise caused by training and drills, accidents, environmental pollution, and crime. Consequently, the presence of the bases has undeniably compromised the everyday lives of the people, inhibited the economic activities of Okinawa, and hampered the vitality and autonomous development of the area.

On the other hand, land from returned bases in the outskirts of cities has been redeveloped as new commercial and/or residential areas. Some examples can be seen in the districts of Kinjo and Ameku in the city of Naha, and in the districts of Hanby and Mihama in the town of Chatan. Land once used for military purposes is valuable to the private sector and enhances the possibilities for urban and economic development. In this way, land currently used by bases like the U.S. Marine Corps' dangerous Futenma Air Station, located in the middle of the city of Ginowan, will be a welcome addition when returned. To promote further development, the U.S. and Japanese governments must continue to reduce and consolidate the U.S. bases, particularly those located in the outskirts of the cities.

(2) ECONOMIC MERITS OF THE VAST BASES ARE DECLINING.

The bases are also of questionable value in macroeconomic terms. Military-related income consists of rent for land occupied by military facilities, income from the bases acting in the capacity of a local employer, and consumer spending of military and civilian personnel and their dependents. However, the total income of local base employees in 2001 was 51 billion yen, rental for land occupied by bases was 84.9 billion yen, and consumer spending by military personnel and military-related persons from the bases was 54.2 billion yen, totaling 190 billion yen. At the time of the reversion to Japan in 1972, military-related receipts were about 78 billion yen, so in absolute terms this represents a 2.4-fold increase. During that period, however, because income in the prefecture increased 7.5-fold since the reversion to 3.7 trillion yen, the ratio of military-related receipts actually decreased from 15.6% at the time of the reversion to 5.6% in 2001. Off-base spending by military and civilian personnel and their dependents, which had benefited the commercial districts in the suburban areas, dropped off significantly (by 35%) with the appreciation of the yen following the Plaza Accord in 1985, creating the impression that the role of bases in the local economy was declining. In addition, rent for land occupied by the bases and the salaries of locally hired base employees are currently paid by the Japanese government under the Host Nation Support arrangements and, in this respect too, the economic significance of the bases is fading. While the bases have been reduced by only 16% in Okinawa, the number of workers employed by U.S. bases has been more than halved from 22,000 at the time of the reversion to just over 8,700 as of March 2002, accounting for only 1.5% of Okinawa's workforce. Consequently, the role of the U.S. bases as a potential employer has been significantly reduced.

Although the economic role of the bases has decreased considerably, it is still the third most important source of revenue, after fiscal-transfer income from the national government (43.7%) and tourism (10.2%). It provides 3.2 times the income derived from agricultural industries, where there is a growing market for orchids, chrysanthemums, vegetables, and tropical fruits like mangoes, and creates income almost on par with the manufacturing industry (185.3 billion yen). Nevertheless, the bases will not resume their former significance as an engine for growth in the Okinawa economy, and U.S. bases and the development of Okinawa's economy are now clearly at odds.

(3) DAMAGES CAUSED BY THE BASES ARE DESTABILIZING THE SOCIETY OF OKINAWA.

All four U.S. military forces — Army, Navy, Air Force, and the Marine Corps — are stationed at American bases in Okinawa. At the end of September 2002, 25,515 military personnel (approximately sixty-three percent of the U.S. military forces stationed in Japan) were based in Okinawa. In addition to military personnel, there were 1,397 civilian personnel and 22,434 dependents, bringing the total to 50,000 people. The distribution among the four services as of September 2002 was as follows: 943 Army; 1,928 Navy; 6,734 Air Force; and 15,910 Marine Corps personnel (sixty-two percent of the total).

With so many U.S. military and civilian personnel and dependents stationed in a small area like Okinawa, it is inevitable that fallout caused by the bases and friction among local residents will occur. Accidents like Air Force plane crashes, emergency landings, noise caused by aircraft, fires caused by live-fire artillery drills, red-earth erosion, pollution of rivers and coastal waters due to waste-oil spills, and other incidents caused by military and military-related personnel are occurring frequently and pose a daily threat to the residents' lives. Statistics for 2002 show the following mishaps and incidents: one airplane crash, fifty-one emergency landings, twelve brush fires, eight water-pollution incidents from waste-oil spills, and eighty-one criminal offenses including heinous crimes. It is noteworthy that about thirty-five percent of the 217 U.S. aircraft accidents occurring since the reversion of Okinawa were caused by aircraft belonging to Futenma Air Station.

The U.S. military presence in Okinawa is an intolerable paradox; U.S. forces, meant to protect Japan from invasion, have instead become a threat to their lives, property, environment, and human rights. The 1995 rape of a young girl by U.S. servicemen in Okinawa clearly shows the enormity of this contradiction. With an income level equal to that of the G-8 countries, the Okinawan people have become sensitive to the unfairness of the bases' excessive burden, the unequal U.S.-Japan Status of Forces Agreement (SOFA), the infringement of their human rights, and the deterioration of their environment. To ensure the stable management of the U.S.-Japan Security Treaty, the U.S. military must make visible efforts to improve the security of the Okinawans by preventing accidents and crimes.

One measure that would improve the situation would be to scale down the bases and the military forces to the allowable minimum for maintaining their strategic functions. Another is to establish fair rules acceptable to the Japanese people for settling crimes and other incidents caused by base operations or personnel. Scaling down the bases and reducing military power — particularly the number of Marine Corps personne — are demands that the Okinawans have been making to the U.S. and Japanese governments and are compelling ways that friction with the local residents could be reduced. Furthermore, with changes in the strategic and security environment since September 11, 2001, the military value of maintaining a large-scale, sixteen-thousand-strong Marine Corps presence in Okinawa is being questioned. Specialists are also doubting whether there is a need to maintain the forward deployment of a one-hundred-thousand-strong military force in the Asia-Pacific region. In the U.S. Defense Department's *Quadrennial Defense Review Report* (QDR) of September 30, 2001, there was no mention of a force of this size, which has led to expectations for a dramatic reorganization and reduction of the Marine Corps in Okinawa.

The SOFA provides for the rights and obligations of the U.S. military forces and personnel. Okinawa, however, as the party bearing the brunt of the bases' cost, has demanded that the Japanese government review the SOFA in regard to extraterritorial rights granted to U.S. military forces and personnel. Japan's House of Representatives' Standing Committee on Foreign Affairs, the National Governors' Association, the Japan Federation of Bar Associations, and Junior Chamber International Japan have adopted resolutions calling for a review of the SOFA. Protest activities are spreading from Okinawa to the main Japanese islands. There is a growing awareness in Japan that the SOFA problem is not uniquely Okinawan; it also involves national sovereignty. The SOFA problem challenges the equality of the U.S.-Japan Security Alliance. The Japanese people now demand the reduction of U.S. military forces in Okinawa and a serious review of the SOFA. These demands have been embodied in the protest against the 1995 rape and the prefecture-wide rally and referendum showing that ninety percent of the Okinawan public is in agreement on these issues, which cannot be overlooked when considering the stability of the U.S.-Japan Security Alliance.

(4) THE BASES ARE DISTORTING MUNICIPAL FINANCES.

Almost sixty years after World War II, the income of the cities and towns and the livelihood of landowners forced to lease property for the bases are still depressed because of the unilateral expropriation of their land. One-third of the U.S. bases are on land owned by the cities and towns, and rental income from the bases increases in proportion to their area. This relationship has resulted in municipal dependency on the bases for a proportion of their income. In 2001, for example, thirty-one of Okinawa's fifty-three cities and towns received 9.3 billion yen for maintenance of areas surrounding the bases, 9.3 billion yen for the lease of base land, 6.5 billion yen in grants, and 6.1 billion yen for other subsidies. This amounted to 31.2 billion yen, equal to 6.6% of the total revenue of the thirty-one cities and towns. Municipalities with the highest dependency on the bases were the town of Kadena (38.8%), the town of Kin (36.6%), the village of Ie (30.1%), the village of Onna (21.8%), the village of Ginoza (18%), and the city of Nago (15%), with a total of ten cities and towns depending on the bases for ten percent or more of their income. These cities and towns face serious problems.

They draw up their budgets based on the assumption of income related to the bases and will not be able to maintain the present level of administrative services if they cannot find alternative sources of income. This dependency on the bases has grown in the half century after the war and has been a factor in reining in those demanding the return of the bases.

The private landowners who have become dependent on rents from the bases face the same problem. One-third of the land used by U.S. bases is privately owned and many landowners derive their livelihood from payments they receive for use of this land. This is particularly true in central Okinawa where many of the important bases are located. In this area, seventy-six percent of the land is privately owned. Okinawan landowners receiving rental income from land leased to bases totaled 36,694 in March 2003. There are an additional 3,300 landowners, members of the One-Tsubo Anti-War Landowners Association, who refuse to accept payment for their land in protest. In 2001, there were 19,266 landowners receiving annual payments of under one million yen (52.5%), 14,123 landowners receiving from one million to less than five million yen (38.5%), and 3,305 landowners receiving five million yen and over (9%). A survey of landowners confirmed that the more rental income they received from base land, the more likely that this income would be their major source of income. Excessive municipal dependence on high-rate land lease revenues is hindering the return of bases and the redevelopment of the resulting vacant land.

Problems in the Approach to the Return of Bases

THE OKINAWA REVERSION AGREEMENT MUST BE REVIEWED.

Like the bases on the main Japanese islands, the legal foundation for the bases in Okinawa after its reversion to Japan in 1972 is provided for in Article Six of the U.S.-Japan Security Treaty. Furthermore, the overall framework concerning the conditions and operation of the bases is established in the Okinawa Reversion Agreement. In the agreement, it was decided that (1) the U.S. bases in Okinawa would be maintained and their military function would not be diminished, and (2) costs for the realignment of the bases would be shouldered by Japan. Moreover, the U.S. Defense Department's East Asia Strategy Report of February 1995 emphasized the value of U.S. military forces in Japan, saying that these forces were not only supporting peace and security in the Asia-Pacific region, but were also influencing an area stretching as far as the Persian Gulf. It also emphasized the Japanese obligation to provide similar alternative facilities in the event that the current bases were returned. Through the U.S.-Japan Security Treaty, the SOFA, and the two provisions cited above in the Okinawa Reversion Agreement, the U.S. not only obtained the right for the continued (free) use of the bases, but also the right to set the terms of relocation if the Japanese government requested the integration or return of bases. Because of the commitments made in the Okinawa Reversion Agreement, the Japanese government has no choice but to accept the relocation within the prefecture of important facilities like Futenma Air Station and Naha Port, the return of which was decided by the Special Action Committee on Okinawa (SACO) Final Report (See Appendix).

Based on the Sato-Nixon joint statement of January 7, 1972, the U.S. military base integration and reduction plan decided by the U.S.-Japan Security Consultative Committee (SCC) has been implemented. While there has been a 60% reduction and integration of bases on the main Japanese islands, there has only been a 16% reduction in Okinawa. As a result, 75% of the land for U.S. bases is concentrated in Okinawa, which makes up only 0.6% of Japan's total land area, thereby placing an extremely unfair burden on the prefecture.

The issue of American base reduction in Okinawa was also taken up by Japan's House of Representatives in November 1971 in a resolution concerning nuclear weapons and the reduction of the U.S. bases in Okinawa. After the reversion of Okinawa, demands by successive prefectural governors have been made ten times to the governments of both Japan and the U.S. In spite of these efforts, the military base issue in Okinawa had been ignored and no serious talks had been held between the U.S. and Japan until the 1995 rape incited a protest against the presence of the bases. The reduction process in Okinawa lagged behind the process in the main Japanese islands, in part because the government had given priority to the reduction and integration of bases in the main islands and had actually ignored the excessive burden of the bases in Okinawa.

As long as strategic bases are maintained in Okinawa, the stability of Okinawa will always be a precondition on which Japanese security, the stability of the U.S.-Japan Security Alliance, and the basis of the countries' bilateral diplomacy are premised. It is also the responsibility of Okinawa, therefore, to demonstrate its ability to represent prefectural interests within the larger context of stability and security. More than any other region, Okinawa requires a balance between domestic politics and foreign diplomacy in security policies. Smooth implementation of the U.S.-Japan Security Treaty will not be possible if the U.S. and Japanese national governments ignore the will of the Okinawan people. The stability of the agreement has been marred by accidents and crimes caused by the U.S. military presence that can at any time develop into protest against the bases. The 1995 rape is one case in point.

RELOCATION WITHIN THE PREFECTURE IS COMPLICATING THE PROCESS.

The SACO Final Report was the first large-scale agreement between the U.S. and Japan concerning the return of bases since Okinawa's reversion to Japan in 1972. Because the agreement stipulates relocation within the prefecture, however, considerable time and an enormous amount of money will be required for the base relocation, the legal arrangements, and the drawing up of local agreements. This will increase the involved municipalities' financial dependence. At the same time, concerns that communities will lose their local autonomy are also surfacing, because the relocation plans and decisions on their contents are being made in Tokyo. Local conflict and social problems arising from the acceptance or rejection of relocation proposals must also be taken into consideration.

The Okinawa Promotion and Development Plans, which began following the 1972 reversion, were established to deal with "the special circumstances" of Okinawa — namely the negative economic impact of the continued presence of U.S. bases. Therefore, in one way, by subsidizing the Okinawan economy, these plans have served as a measure for maintaining the bases. After the 1995 rape, a special allowance, apart from the existing budget for the Promotion and Development Plans from the Okinawa Development Agency, was allocated in consideration of the excessive burden the bases place on Okinawa. In addition, an annual special adjustment fund of ten billion yen for a period of ten years, totaling one hundred billion yen, was earmarked for revitalization projects in cities and towns where bases are located.

Costs estimated for base relocation in the northern region development projects are estimated at about one hundred billion yen over ten years. When including other costs associated with relocation under the SACO Final Report, a rough estimate puts the total at over one trillion yen. This gives us an idea of how relocation complicates the political and social processes of the return of the bases.

The Problem of Creating a More Self-reliant Economy

OKINAWA'S ECONOMIC DEPENDENCE ON GOVERNMENT FUNDS IS SERIOUS.

Gross product in Okinawa grew in real terms from 605.7 billion yen in 1972 to 3,599.8 billion yen in 2001. This represents a 6-fold increase, which is more than 2.4 times higher than real national growth. Per capita income in the prefecture went from 440,000 yen at the time of the 1972 reversion to 2.06 million yen in 2001, showing a 4.7-fold increase. Even though the population of Okinawa increased at a rate 2 times the national average during this period, per capita income also rose from 61% to 71% of the national average. Okinawa's per capita income level remains the lowest among Japan's forty-seven prefectures, but is equivalent to US$19,600 in real terms, which is greater than the average income level of four of the G-8 Summit participant countries ($18,800 for Britain, Germany, France, and Italy).

While at a glance this shows the dramatic growth the Okinawan economy has achieved, at the same time this growth depended largely on transfer income from the national government. Local infrastructure improved dramatically as a result of enormous government investment designed to reduce the disparity between Okinawa and the main Japanese islands and maintain the U.S. bases following the 1972 reversion. In the private sector economy, however, there are few promising industries that could become an engine for economic growth other than tourism. Okinawa is in a situation where economic expansion is impossible without public fiscal contributions.

Although gross income in the twenty-nine years between the 1972 reversion and 2001 grew 7.5-fold to 3,794 billion yen, the driving force behind this growth was government fiscal appropriations. Public spending, base-related income, and tourism have been called Okinawa's three engines of growth and account for 43.7%, 5.1%, and 10.2% of the prefecture's total economy respectively. At the time of reversion in 1972, those figures were 23.5%, 15.6%, and 8.1%. Industries like tourism, health foods, flowering plants, and tropical fruits have grown, but the overall degree of fiscal autonomy is in decline. Public funds, channeled through enormous fiscal transfers, are maintaining the industrial structure bloated by tertiary industries, covering the huge trade imbalance, and making Okinawa's economic cycles possible. All self-sufficiency indicators — fiscal dependence (public expenditures / gross expenditures in the prefecture), physical productive capacity [(total primary industry production + total industrial and mining production) / total prefectural production], the external balance coefficient (exports / imports), and regional self-sufficiency [(1- inbound products + imports) / total demand in the prefecture] — have deteriorated since Okinawa's reversion. The reason the local economy has not gone bankrupt, however, is because of the government's fund transfers.

THE NATIONAL GOVERNMENT'S POLICIES FOR CREATING A SELF-RELIANT ECONOMY ARE NOT WORKING.

The government's industrial promotion policies have not been successful to date. Protected agricultural products like pineapples and sugarcane have declined, but products exposed to competition like flowering plants, tropical fruits, and vegetables have enjoyed growth. The tourism industry grew amidst market competition, but policies promoting industry and trade including a free trade zone, industrial development districts, and other incentives have produced no lasting results. The new programs introduced in the latter half of the Third Okinawa Promotion and Development Plan — including a special free trade zone, tourism promotion zones, information and communications industry zones, incentives like the special finance district, and corporate tax reductions and investment tax breaks — were poorly planned programs inferior to incentive measures of neighboring countries. In terms of cost, whether it be labor, raw material, land, transport, utility, or production, there are no conditions under which Okinawa can compete with the surrounding countries or regions. The new programs' preferential measures were not well designed and did not provide successful incentives to promote industry.

To give one example, tourism is considered a promising industry for Okinawa, yet the Tourism Promotion Zone initiatives that are supposed to foster the industry exclude from its incentive program vital accommodation facilities like hotels. Retail sales facilities also must be on a large scale, three thousand square meters or more, to qualify for incentives. For tourism resort enterprises located in rural areas where demand is low, large retail facilities are not viable. The measures do not, therefore, provide incentives for establishing businesses. In another tourism initiative, measures were taken to reduce airport fuel taxes and arrival charges to attract tourists with reduced airfares. Since the deregulation of airfares, however, the effectiveness of these measures has all but evaporated. Similar criticism can be leveled at a number of other development measures and any reported successes at fostering self-sufficient industries are viewed with suspicion. We must ask why the government continues to forward plans of this sort where results cannot be expected.

Proposals

Because strategic bases are located in Okinawa, the problems they pose are strongly colored by various conflicting interests that include Japanese national interests, the United States' global power interests, and Okinawa's regional interests. Making satisfactory adjustments depends on the overall power of the parties and their ability to negotiate. Okinawa is demanding that Japan be fair in its treatment of the region; Japan is asking the U.S. to treat it as an equal partner in the U.S.-Japan Security Alliance; and the U.S. seems to be advancing its own global strategy — using the U.S.-Japan Security Treaty and the Okinawa Reversion Agreement as its shield. The ultimate challenge, however, is to create a new, shared vision for the future that will shape a framework to resolve the problems posed by the bases and establish a self-reliant Okinawan economy.

I will not go into detail about that vision for the future, but it is based on a concept that will transform Okinawa from a strategic military foothold (hard power) to a non-military foothold (soft power) for creating Japan's new national identity for the twenty-first century and a framework for an Asia-Pacific community based on peace, stability, and prosperity. At the same time, it will be based on the common understanding that the U.S.-Japan Security Treaty contributes to the peace, security, and prosperity of Japan and the Asia-Pacific region as a whole.

A PROPOSAL FOR THE REDUCTION OF OKINAWA'S BASES.

The SACO Final Report stipulates a return of twenty-one percent of the total land used by the U.S. military in Okinawa (excluding jointly used bases). Even with full implementation, however, the percentage of U.S. military exclusively-used land in Japan that is in Okinawa will only be reduced by five percent, from seventy-five to seventy percent, far from the significant consolidation and reduction of bases demanded by the Okinawan people. This is because conditions for relocating within the prefecture were attached to most of the eleven facilities tapped for reduction and realignment, including Futenma. It is hard to deny that the Okinawa Reversion Agreement is the cause of the problem.

Secondly, gaining approval from residents living near the proposed relocation area for Futenma has consumed an enormous amount of time and money. Even now, as the promised five-to-seven-year deadline for Futenma's return has passed, there are still unresolved problems hindering construction. It is estimated that the environmental impact assessment (started in 2003) will take three years and construction will take at least ten years, making the Futenma relocation possible in thirteen years at the earliest, even after the proposal clears the prefectural government's condition of a fifteen-year usage limit. Since this usage limit must be addressed before the start of construction, residents near the current Futenma Air Station will continue to share the high risks of the base, considered to be the most dangerous of all the U.S. facilities in Japan, together with both the governments of Japan and the U.S. for at least thirteen more years.

Thirdly, demands for a fifteen-year usage limit and a joint military-civilian air facility are two of the cards Okinawa can play to prevent permanent base relocation within the prefecture and to develop a self-reliant economy. When considering at least thirteen years for the environmental impact assessment and construction, and fifteen years for the actual usage, this time limit will actually be settled in approximately thirty years. While the security environment thirty years in the future cannot be predicted, it is clear that the heavy burden of American bases should not be shouldered by Okinawa alone.

Fourthly, in the context of the revolution in military affairs (RMA), the U.S. Defense Department and the U.S. Congress are working to reorganize, consolidate, and dismantle American bases overseas. Although this policy's influence on U.S. bases in Japan is not yet clear, it is possible that various options involving forces in Japan will be proposed before construction is started on the Futenma relocation facility. The prefectural government should not, therefore, ignore other options like the recently reported possibility of relocating bases to the main Japanese islands or overseas, the provisional relocation of Futenma's squadrons to Kadena Air Base, or unconditional reversion, while continuing to promote the SACO Final Report. It is important to pursue these other options, because the current relocation site is within a protected environmental area offshore of Nago's Henoko district and building on it should be avoided if possible. Additionally, it must be stressed that the latest development plan started in July 2002, the Fourth Okinawa Promotion and Development Plan, designates neighboring Kin Bay for important resort development.

The terrorist acts of 9/11, the wars in Afghanistan and Iraq, other global threats, and advances in high-tech weapons systems demand that major changes in the Asia-Pacific security environment be made. Doubts are being raised particularly in regard to the United States' concept of forward deployment. Shouldn't the Japanese government also demand a review of the U.S. bases in Okinawa in hopes of lightening the excessive burden the bases place on the prefecture? It must be noted that base reduction and realignment are stated explicitly in the Fourth Okinawa Promotion and Development Plan.

PROPOSAL FOR BUILDING A SELF-RELIANT ECONOMY.

As long as the bases exist in Okinawa, prefectural dependence on national government financing will remain and a self-sufficient economy cannot be expected to develop. If, for example, a self-reliant economy were defined as having a lower level (twenty-two percent of the national average) of dependence on government financing while maintaining the same economic standard (prefectural GDP or gross domestic income), Okinawa would have to create a further 690 billion yen in private sector demand. Since even the tourism industry, which has grown rapidly in the period following the reversion of Okinawa, has not yet reached the level of 500 billion yen, this goal is highly unrealistic. Because the national government adopts policies that favor the bases and dependence on government financing, and since the cities and towns use the bases to secure their municipal budgets, it will be hard to develop economic self-reliance.

Okinawa cannot succeed in developing a self-reliant economy under the existing system. The current framework promotes Okinawan development through policies linked to public works, military bases, and nationally administered programs, through padding the ratio of assistance funds, and through alternate measures by the national government for prefectural and municipal projects. Okinawa will not be able to escape from its dependence on national government financing, because the current system is not based on autonomous decisions and responsibility. If we move toward a system where the prefecture can secure and freely use a budget with no strings attached, the prefecture itself can work out optimal industrial policies for its own infant industries and take positive steps toward self-reliance. Of course, the final responsibility rests with Okinawa.

[1] The White House Office of the Press Secretary , "Transcript: Remarks by President Clinton to the People of Okinawa," Cornerstone of Peace Park, Okinawa, Japan, 21 July 2000.

[2] Kurayoshi Takara, Tsuneo Oshiro, Morisada Maeshiro, "Toward an 'Okinawa Initiative' — A Possible Role for Okinawa in Asia Pacific," *Community Building in Asia Pacific: Dialogue in Okinawa*, Japan Center for International Exchange, Tokyo, June 2002.

[3] Military Base Affairs Office, Okinawa Prefectural Government, *U.S. Military Bases in Okinawa*, 2004 Edition.

Citizen Interests and the U.S. Military Presence in Asia:
Okinawa in Comparative Perspective

Sheila A. Smith
The East-West Center

T he U.S. has maintained military forces in the Asia-Pacific region since the end of World War II, and its alliances with key countries in the region continue today to be seen as critical to regional peace and stability. These alliances, like NATO in Europe, were instigated by the Cold War, and with its demise governments have had to reconsider alliance goals and policies. Regional stability became the goal of Asia's alliances, and the U.S. military presence in Asia was viewed by Washington and allied governments alike as the key to communicating U.S. interests in the security equation in Asia. Despite massive draw downs of U.S. forces deployed in Europe in the 1990s, U.S. forces in the Asia-Pacific region remained virtually unchanged at around 100,000 personnel.

If allied governments were convinced that the U.S. military should stay in Asia, their citizens were not. Even before the Cold War formally came to a close, the call for constraining the U.S. military and its operations was being heard from within allied societies. In New Zealand, the public call for limiting the U.S. Navy's ability to bring nuclear weapons into national ports led to a virtual end to the ANZUS pact in the mid-1980s. In 1991, the Philippine Senate rejected a revised security treaty, and the U.S. was asked to close its two regional bases there, the U.S. Air Force's Clark Air Base and the Navy's Subic Naval Base.

The last half of the 1990s brought intense public criticism even in Washington's most stalwart allies: Japan and South Korea. In both societies, the behavior of U.S. military forces triggered intense episodes of public antagonism towards the U.S. military, and created crises for alliance policymakers on both sides of the Pacific Ocean. The 1995 rape of a twelve-year-old schoolgirl by U.S. servicemen in Okinawa resulted in calls for the withdrawal of U.S. forces from the prefecture, and set in motion a longer-term process of negotiation between local and national governments of the terms of the U.S. troop presence in Japan's southernmost prefecture. Rumblings of discontent in South Korea resulted in a renegotiation of the bilateral Status of Forces Agreement (SOFA), but the country exploded in anger towards the United States in 2002 after two young girls were killed by an American military vehicle as they walked home from school. Months later, a verdict of "not guilty" for those U.S. personnel responsible for the accident sparked massive demonstrations and a striking outpouring of "anti-Americanism" that fueled the election of a new president, Roh Moo-hyun, who wondered aloud about the necessity of U.S. forces in South Korea.

With an intensity that had not been seen for decades, we have witnessed political leaders willing to challenge the way in which these alliances had been managed in the past. The U.S. military presence became a focal point of national politics. In both Japan and South Korea, U.S. bases became the topic for electoral contest, civil society activists mobilized to call for troop reductions and/or withdrawals, and local citizens organized to demonstrate against the status quo. New avenues of political advocacy were available in both Japan and South Korea, much as they had been in Manila years earlier, and it became imperative that Washington find new ways of responding to citizen complaints. In both cases, the timing was key. In 1995, outspoken Okinawa Governor Masahide Ota successfully challenged the national government's approach to base policy at a critical moment in the redefinition of the U.S.-Japan Security Alliance. And, the intensity of South Korean sentiment over the U.S.-South Korea alliance and the future of the Korean Peninsula resulted in the election of President Roh Moo-hyun who openly questioned the value of the U.S. military presence.

The Domestic Politics of the U.S. Military Presence

Security policy, like any other realm of public policy, is subject to domestic political activism and interest articulation. And yet, after half a century or more of the U.S. military presence in Asia, we still have little appreciation for the constellation of interests, and the avenues of interest articulation, that shape U.S. alliances in the region. The story of each bilateral alliance includes past moments of protest such as these, and ultimately the dynamics of protest come into focus the most clearly when the diplomatic agendas of the U.S. and its ally are disrupted. In

Japan, for example, the most memorable public protest against the alliance came in 1960 when mass demonstrations in Tokyo over the government's handling of the revision of the U.S.-Japan Security Treaty caused President Dwight Eisenhower to cancel his visit due to security concerns.

Moreover, when studied nationally, episodes of protest and contention over the U.S. military presence seem best understood in the context of the domestic politics of the moment. The intensity of protest is often a function of domestic currents of political change. In the early 1970s, a national anti-war movement joined forces with longstanding anti-base activism in Okinawa over the use of U.S. bases there for bombing runs to North Vietnam, and convinced many that Japan needed to regain sovereignty over the Ryukyu Islands as soon as possible. In South Korea, anti-base sentiment has also been fused with anti-government protest as successive national leaders clamped down on those who stood up against them. Finally, the Philippine "people's power" movement and the challenge to Ferdinand Marcos was clearly the backdrop against the effort to inject greater national voice into the bilateral security treaty deliberations with Washington.

Public concern and questioning of the U.S. military presence is not a new phenomenon, and while the end of the Cold War has produced a new context for evaluating the U.S. military presence, the shadow of the past extends much further back. The circumstances under which the U.S. began its postwar security relationship with each of its Asian allies were markedly different. The imprimatur of war and occupation in the case of Japan and South Korea, and the longer experience of U.S. colonialism in the Philippines, created a tension that continues today to color public perceptions of national policies regarding the U.S. military. Over the decades since, national governments were repeatedly asked to demonstrate their ability to represent their own citizens' interests which were often in opposition to Washington's strategic priorities. The common theme of compromised sovereignty infused the national debate in Japan, South Korea, and the Philippines.

In each of these very different societies, the more mundane issues that affected the daily lives of citizens were surprisingly similar. Many, particularly those that lived in proximity to U.S. military bases, worried that their governments would be unable to exercise discretion over the aims and the use of U.S. military forces. Of particular concern in Japan and New Zealand were the use and the deployment of nuclear weapons. And most importantly, the behavior of U.S. troops in allied societies occasioned the most heated criticism. Criminal behavior by U.S. forces attracted the sharpest condemnation, and often produced demands for compensation and appeals for greater national control over the behavior of U.S. military personnel.

Managing the alliances, therefore, requires more than a strategic assessment of the need for U.S. military forces. In fact, the complexity of the impacts of the U.S. presence on host societies reveals the multiple aspects of basing policy that affect national government efforts to address domestic grievances. Okinawa has been the location of major U.S. military bases for more than half a century now, and its experience suggests that new approaches to considering this problem are required. More than a strategic policy, the U.S. military presence has become a social policy, and it is from this vantage point that U.S. allied societies consider the question of whether or not, and in what form, the U.S. military should remain in Asia.

Citizen Complaint and the "Extraterritoriality" of Status of Forces Agreements (SOFAs)

Public sensitivity to the presence of "foreign troops" is at its highest when U.S. military personnel are involved in accidents or commit crimes that harm host nation communities. The SOFAs crafted to set forth the terms of managing this foreign force are seen primarily as administrative documents by Washington, but for the citizens of U.S. allies, SOFAs represent a Cold War "extraterritoriality" that pits national security interests against citizen welfare.

Criminal behavior and the procedures for dealing with U.S. military personnel accused of crimes overseas are the most contentious aspects of the SOFAs. Moreover, the irritation occasioned by SOFAs and their implementation are exacerbated by the fact that these agreements differ from country to country. Early on in the history of the U.S.-Japan Security Alliance, the implementation of its SOFA was severely tested. In 1957, a celebrated case of murder by a U.S. serviceman caused intense scrutiny of the alliance. A U.S. soldier shot an elderly Japanese woman who had been collecting spent shell casings on a firing range. In the testimony of witnesses, it became clear that this soldier had taunted Japanese villagers, urging them onto the range only then to take shots at them. This case, referred to as the Girard Case, resulted in the first U.S. decision to transfer a soldier to Japanese police custody, and to allow him to be tried in Japanese courts.

The Girard Case did not produce a renegotiation of the SOFA, but it did create a precedent for bilateral handling of criminal cases. Moreover, it produced a U.S. judicial review of the SOFAs in the United States. When the U.S. Defense Department agreed to transfer Private William Girard to Japanese custody, his family took the U.S. government to court, accusing the U.S. of abandoning his civil protections. The case moved expeditiously to the U.S. Supreme Court

Around sixteen thousand protestors form a human chain completely around the U.S. Marine Corps Futenma Air Station on May 16, 2004, asking for an early return of the base. (Okinawa Times)

for complex technical reasons, but the important point is that the Supreme Court for the first time in the Cold War decided in favor of the U.S. government's ability to use its discretion in deciding criminal jurisdiction issues in "foreign" courts.

More recently, the implementation of criminal prosecution in the U.S.-Japan Security Alliance continues to attract attention. After the 1995 rape in Okinawa, the U.S. and Japanese governments again sought to respond to citizen outrage by changing the way that they implemented the transfer of custody of U.S. military personnel in the case of "heinous crimes." Transfer of custody prior to indictment would become possible in cases where the nature of the crime warranted it, but also where the evidence possessed by Japanese and U.S. military authorities was consistent with an indictment. In recent cases involving U.S. personnel in Okinawa since the 1995 rape, this aspect of the U.S. policy has again come to the forefront of the policy debate. There is significant interest in revisiting this policy amendment to clarify the timing and the circumstances of turning over U.S. military personnel. But there is also a danger that this will create new opportunities for challenging the U.S. government's obligation to its military personnel, and in a recent case, a U.S. Marine Corps officer accused of attempted rape openly charged that the U.S. government violated his constitutional rights by handing him over to Japanese prosecutors.

This penchant for reinterpreting the implementation of the SOFA in the U.S.-Japan Security Alliance has thus far served the interests of the U.S. and Japanese governments well. Calls for revision of the SOFA remain, however. Local governors in Kanagawa Prefecture and Okinawa Prefecture have openly called for revision, and some national lawmakers have taken up the issue. This question of revising the terms of SOFAs, agreements conceived and negotiated under considerably different international and domestic political circumstances, remains a sensitive one for all governments that host U.S. forces. Changes in South Korean domestic laws, particularly those related to the environment, prompted a reconsideration of the terms of that SOFA, and there is still some interest in South Korea of addressing some of the more complicated issues related to criminal prosecution.

Local Economic Development and U.S. Military Bases

Okinawa's experience is perhaps most pressing when it comes to the impact of U.S. military bases on local economic development. For half a century, the U.S. and Japanese governments have pursued a policy of providing economic rewards — either formal or informal — to those communities that host U.S. bases. The result, of course, has been to create and sustain economic reliance on the bases within host communities. To the extent that these communities have alternative resources, or alternative avenues of generating local revenue, these interests can be less than determinant when it comes time to think about consolidating or even removing bases.

Citizen interests regarding the U.S. military presence are divided in most communities. The conspicuous presence of U.S. forces in national capitals — such as the Kanto area in Japan in the 1970s and Seoul today in South Korea — was an irritant that affected most citizens. Not only were these "foreign" troops a reminder of compromised sovereignty, but they were also occupying prime metropolitan land. Land values, commercial interests, and the visibility of this "foreign" presence make it very difficult to sustain popular support for presence. Most U.S. bases, however, are located in more isolated and even rural settings where the economic benefits are clearer than the lost opportunities. Jobs are created, small businesses are needed, and national subsidies are provided for the communities that host U.S. forces. Economic interests are created and shaped around the bases over time, and many in the community have a direct or at least indirect economic interest in sustaining the U.S. presence.

But when the time comes to move a U.S. base, or even to reduce and consolidate the "footprint" of U.S. forces, these interests become barriers to change. Alternative mechanisms for generating local revenue are needed, and in the case of Okinawa, the legal terms for transitioning land from military to civilian use offer landowners mixed incentives for post-base land conversion. A longer-term version of national government support for landowners will undoubtedly be needed over time, particularly if U.S. force restructuring proceeds. In larger and more developed communities, the question of what to do with the massive tracts of land left behind by U.S. forces presents national and local governments with significant policy challenges. The case of Subic Naval Base in the Philippines initially offered an optimistic glimpse of the possibilities for commercial development as Richard Gordon, an enterprising mayor of the city of Olongapo, sought to create a regional commercial transportation hub out of the U.S. base.

Okinawa's planning experience, however, suggests that this is the exception rather than the rule. Private sector capital is not uniformly available or interested in taking over from governments. Without massive private capital, however, there is little that local communities can do. Environmental degradation of larger facilities, such as the U.S. Marine Corps' Futenma Air Station, will make civilian habitation impossible. National government planning for base conversion in Okinawa will be a crucial factor in translating the current topography of U.S. bases there into a more manageable living space for Okinawa's residents.

In short, the national government created many of the economic dependencies visible today in Okinawa, and a new partnership will need to be developed that will translate these base-related dependencies into a more viable partnership for economic growth if U.S. forces are to be consolidated, and reduced, over time.

Changing Norms of Democratic Practice

In all of the societies allied with the U.S. in the Asia-Pacific region, domestic political change is affecting the issue of the U.S. military presence in unpredictable ways. A cross-national comparison of Japan, South Korea, and the Philippines reveals that there are broader sets of issues — often unrelated to security policymaking — that affect public reaction and response to the U.S. bases. Similar challenges confront national leaders who must manage their alliances with the United States and respond to citizen concerns about the presence of U.S. soldiers on their soil. These are all democratic societies, although this was not always the case. And yet the extent to which citizens determine their governments and the extent to which these governments are responsive to citizen concerns differ greatly.

Common themes do emerge, however. The communities most affected by the U.S. military presence are often far from the center of political power, and indeed some citizens, e.g., women, are marginalized even in the local policymaking process on the bases. Today, however, there are broader transformations within these societies that bring new interests, new faces, and new positions of advocacy to the fore. Instead of being motivated by security policy goals and concerns, these new voices in the debate over the bases frequently frame their complaints in terms of women's rights, environmental degradation, and land claims.

Moreover, the growing transnational reach of local civil society groups suggests that the sharing of information, strategies, and tactics for opposing unacceptable base policies is playing an increasingly influential role across the Asia-Pacific region. Local politicians travel from Okinawa to the Philippines, or to Korea, and vice versa to consider how other societies manage the presence of "foreign troops." We still do not have a full understanding of how this cross-national learning affects social movements across national boundaries, but both civil society and national and local governments are increasingly seeing the U.S. base issue as a transnational issue rather than one to be handled via the national political process.

Yet, it is also clear that even in democratic societies, the privileged place of security and foreign policy on the national policy agenda remains an exceptional one. The "national interest" variously defined and keenly contested ultimately sets the stage for the formulation and implementation of security policy. For societies that rely on "foreign troops" and on negotiated security assistance from the U.S., the debate over national interest is more complex. More importantly, however, the relationship between citizen and government is further distanced by a policymaking process that subjugates the interests of particular groups of citizens to the "national" interest in security. Much of the citizen advocacy that we see today, especially that emanating from Okinawa and from South Korea, reveals that national governments are having difficulty in meeting citizen demands for accountability, and as a result, the U.S. military presence can severely strain state-society relations at critical moments of policy change.

Okinawa's Challenge to Alliance Policymakers

Citizen voices are now integral to the national debates over U.S. forces stationed in Asian societies. Citizens from vastly different countries are demonstrating their displeasure with the status of U.S. military forces and bases within their societies, and they are using the instruments of national democratic practice to register their concerns: elections, referendums, and at times, demonstrations in the street. There is also increasing access to information outside of the local and national contexts within which these issues have been debated. Transnational learning among citizen groups in Okinawa, Seoul, and the Philippines is clearly on the rise, and this will clearly impact the way citizens articulate their interests.

Government arguments for the strategic value of the alliances with the United States seem persuasive at the macro level. But government policies to deal with the local policy issues associated with the U.S. military presence seem insufficient to address citizen interests. In other words, the strategic rationale for the U.S. presence may be appreciated, but the social consequences — the costs as opposed to the benefits — may be increasingly the focal point of public attention.

It is here that Okinawa offers the greatest challenge to alliance policymakers:

- long history of divided opinion within the prefecture
- constellation of contending economic interests which require new approaches to long-term economic development planning
- negotiated change and the policymaking process

The social impact of half a century of U.S. military presence in Okinawa is considerable, and has significant implications for how we understand the future of the U.S. military's relationship with the citizens of the Asia-Pacific region. Rather than seeing the question as simply a strategic assessment of operational needs, the basing of U.S. forces in the region — and the force posture restructuring that many imagine is in the making — needs a broader framework for resolution. Governments in Washington, Tokyo, and Okinawa will all need to participate in a planning process that addresses the social impact of the bases and the need for a comprehensive plan for transforming and restructuring the interests of Okinawan residents. In addition, this plan will need to incorporate citizen stakeholders, as well as national security planners.

Military Transformation
and Regional Security

Modernizing the U.S. Military— and Other Nato Forces:
Implications for the Asia-Pacific Region

Michael O'Hanlon

The Brookings Institution

I n the current American defense debate, discussions of modernizing the armed forces' weapons, combat units, and warfighting doctrine generally are motivated by the hypothesis that a revolution in military affairs (RMA) of historical significance is attainable. Even for skeptics of this hypothesis, the debate is useful, for it helps organize discussions of military modernization conceptually. Otherwise they can quickly degenerate into a weapon-by-weapon assessment of the marginal value of this or that procurement program. Such analysis remains important, but lacks thematic structure and makes it difficult to evaluate one type of proposed weapon system against another. That said, careful examination of the RMA/defense transformation hypothesis suggests that it is often overstated and that many of its prescriptions could do more harm than good. Moreover, those proponents of revolutionary change who felt frustrated by what they saw as the slow pace of technical and doctrinal innovation in the U.S. military in the 1990s should probably reconsider, in light of the spectacular performance of coalition forces in Afghanistan in 2001 and Iraq in 2003.

U.S. spending on military acquisition—that is, the sum of the procurement account and the research, development, testing, and evaluation (RDT&E) account—must increase in the years ahead. Equipment purchased primarily during President Ronald Reagan's defense buildup is beginning to wear out en bloc and simply must be replaced. That said, there is a great deal of room for disagreement about which weapons should be purchased, the relative importance of RDT&E spending versus procurement spending, and the amount by which acquisition spending must increase.

There is a strong argument that defense revolutionaries are on strongest footing when they promote greater use of modern electronics rather than haste to continually replace and modernize large weapons platforms. That perspective leads to a philosophy of purchasing "silver bullet" forces of advanced weaponry, rather than pursuing the U.S. Defense Department's current aspirations to replace most existing U.S. weaponry with next-generation and highly expensive systems. Aging equipment would otherwise be replaced by purchasing existing technologies — F-16s for F-16s, and so forth. This approach would be partly motivated by cost considerations; even if the Defense Department's annual budget increases in the years ahead, it is unlikely to expand by the $30 to $50 billion needed to fund the existing force and procurement program. But it is also motivated by the conviction that current trends in technology argue for a relative emphasis on electronics, sensors, advanced munitions, automation, and joint-service experimentation rather than traditional military platforms.

Similar conclusions follow for European militaries, which — like the U.S. Marine Corps — need to establish clear priorities to guide their weapons purchases. Their modest acquisition budgets do not permit pursuit of all RMA agendas at once. They should emphasize advanced electronic technologies more than new planes, ships, and vehicles.

The Contemporary Revolution in Military Affairs Debate

Due to the excellent performance of American high-technology weapons in the Persian Gulf War of 1991, as well as the phenomenal pace of innovation in the modern computer industry, many defense analysts posited in the 1990s that an RMA was either imminent or already underway. The RMA thesis holds that further advances in precision munitions, real-time data dissemination, and other modern technologies, together with associated changes in warfighting organizations and doctrines, can help transform the nature of future war and with it, the size and structure of the U.S. military as well as allied forces. RMA proponents believe that military technology, and the resultant potential for radically new types of warfighting tactics and strategies, is advancing at a rate unrivaled since the 1920s through 1940s, when blitzkrieg, aircraft carriers, large-scale amphibious and airborne assault, ballistic missiles, strategic bombing, and nuclear weapons were developed.

In the abstract, it is unobjectionable to favor innovation. But the prescriptions of some RMA proponents would have major opportunity costs. RMA proponents tend to argue that more budgetary resources should be devoted to innovation — research and development (R&D), procurement of new hardware, frequent experiments with new technology — and, to the extent necessary, less money to military operations, training, and readiness. To free up funds for an RMA transformation strategy, some would reduce U.S. global engagement and weaken the military's deterrent posture.[1]

Some have argued that a radical transformation of the U.S. military will save money.[2] But that argument is unconvincing, at least for the short to medium term. Transformation means accelerating replacement of existing equipment, and while it is theoretically possible that doing so could produce smaller, less expensive units wielding highly advanced and effective weaponry, there is little practical evidence that such an outcome is achievable in the near term.

Given the budgetary and opportunity costs associated with rapidly pursuing an RMA and the popularity of the RMA concept in the contemporary defense debate, some caution is in order. Before developing a modernization agenda, it is worth remembering what can go wrong with a rush to transform — and what innovations can occur even if no RMA is formally declared or pursued.

Reasons Not to Rush an RMA

History provides ample grounds for caution about pursuing major defense transformation. Most contemporary RMA enthusiasts make reference to the interwar years and claim that we are in another period of similar potential, promise, and peril today. However, military technology advanced steadily and impressively throughout the twentieth century, including its latter half. Helicopters radically reshaped many battlefield operations after World War II. Intercontinental ballistic missiles (ICBMs) and space-launch vehicles followed. Satellite communications were first used militarily in 1965 in Vietnam, where aircraft-delivered, precision-guided munitions also made their debut in the early 1970s. Air defense and antitank missiles played major roles in the 1973 Arab-Israeli War. Stealth fighters were designed in the late 1970s.[3] Infrared sensors and night-vision technologies made their debut in this period as well.

History also tells us that radical military transformations only make sense when technology and new concepts and tactics are ripe. At other times, targeted modernizations together with vigorous research, development, and experimentation make more sense. A good analogy is the period of the 1920s, when major military vehicles and systems such as the tank and airplane were not yet ready for large-scale purchase. In addition, advanced operational concepts such as blitzkrieg and carrier aviation had not yet been fully developed in a manner that could guide hardware acquisition or the reshaping of military organizations. As such, research, prototyping, and experimentation were the proper elements of a wise innovation and acquisition strategy. In the 1930s, new operational concepts were better understood, technologies better developed, and geostrategic circumstances more foreboding. Under these circumstances, large-scale modernization made sense, and those countries that did not conduct it tended to perform badly in the early phases of World War II. Because most RMA proponents cannot clearly specify what a near-term transformation should consist of, I am inclined to liken today's situation to the 1920s rather than the 1930s.

It is far from obvious that military technology is now poised to advance even more quickly than it has in the last half century. Yet RMA proponents assert that it will when they call for a radical transformation strategy for current U.S. armed forces. No such Defense Department-wide transformation strategies were necessary to bring satellites, stealth aircraft, precision-guided munitions, advanced jet engines, night-vision equipment, or other remarkable new capabilities into the force in past decades.[4] And defense revolutionaries were generally frustrated by the pace of change during the 1990s — even though, with the hindsight of the recent wars in Afghanistan and Iraq, it now appears that a relatively non-radical philosophy towards innovation during the last decade nonetheless produced some very impressive capabilities.

RMA proponents are certainly right to believe that a successful military must always be changing. But the post-World War II U.S. military has already taken that adage to heart. The status quo in defense circles does not mean standing still; it means taking a balanced approach to modernization that has served the country remarkably well for decades.

Moreover, radical innovation is not always good. If the wrong ideas are adopted, transforming a force can make it worse. For example, in the world wars, militaries overestimated the likely effects of artillery as well as aerial and battleship bombardment against prepared defensive positions, meaning that their infantry forces proved much more vulnerable than expected when they assaulted enemy lines.[5] Britain's radically new all-tank units were inflexible, making them less successful than Germany's integrated mechanized divisions in World War II. Strategic aerial bombardment did not achieve nearly the results that had been expected of it; airpower was much more effective as close-air support for armored formations in blitzkrieg operations.[6] Later on, the U.S. Army's Pentomic division concept, intended to employ tactical nuclear weapons, was adopted for a time and then abandoned in 1961.[7]

A sign warns against entering the U.S. Air Force's Kadena Air Base. (Dennis T. Nakasone)

But these are only historical arguments, uninformed by the realities of today's world. Current trends in defense technology, and the potential for corresponding innovations in tactics and doctrine, are what will really determine the prospects for a near-term RMA. These trends suggest that the technological case for a patient, targeted approach is much more compelling than that for a radical remaking of the U.S. armed forces more generally.

One type of evidence to support this argument is that, despite their haste to push the revolution along, radical RMA promoters tend to lack clear and specific proposals for how to do so. In that light, even if they are right that an RMA may be within reach sometime in the foreseeable future, they may be quite wrong about what should be done about it in the near future. In practical terms, there is a major distinction between the early stages of a possible RMA and the later stages. As Stephen Rosen writes, "The general lesson for students or advocates of innovation may well be that it is wrong to focus on budgets when trying to understand or promote innovation. Bringing innovations to fruition will often be expensive. Aircraft carriers, fleets of helicopters, and ICBM forces were not cheap. But initiating an innovation and bringing it to the point where it provides a strategically useful option has been accomplished when money was tight.... Rather than money, talented military personnel, time, and information have been the key resources for innovation."[8]

Some individuals feel that the above arguments notwithstanding, the United States really has no choice but to rebuild its equipment inventories and combat units from first principles. They believe that future adversaries will make greater use of sea mines, cruise and ballistic missiles, chemical or biological weapons, and other means to attempt to deny the U.S. military the ability to build up forces and operate from large, fixed infrastructures as in the Persian Gulf War of 1991. As a result, they consider major changes in the way U.S. armed forces deploy and fight to be essential.

However, many of the solutions to these problems may not be in the realm of advanced weaponry. True, long-range strike platforms, missile defenses, short-takeoff aircraft, and other such advanced technologies may be part of the appropriate response. But so might more minesweepers, smaller roll-on/roll-off transport vessels useful in shallow ports, concrete bunkers for deployed aircraft, and other relatively low-tech approaches to hardening and dispersing supplies and infrastructure. The military services already are biased in favor of procuring advanced weaponry at the expense of equally important but less advanced hardware. By emphasizing modernistic and futuristic technology, the most ambitious RMA concepts could reinforce this existing tendency, quite possibly to the nation's detriment.

Most centrally, one should be skeptical about the RMA hypothesis, because many of its key technical underpinnings have not been well established and may not be valid. Proponents of the RMA concept often make passing mention of Moore's law — the trend for the number of transistors that can fit on a semiconductor chip to double every eighteen to twenty-four months — and then extrapolate such a radical rate of progress to much different realms of technology. For example, in its 1997 report the National Defense Panel wrote, "The rapid rate of new and improved technologies — a new cycle about every eighteen months — is a defining characteristic of this era of change and will have an indelible influence on new strategies, operational concepts, and tactics that our military employs."[9] However, conflating progress in computers with progress in other major areas of technology is unjustified. To the extent RMA believers hinge most of their argument on advances in modern electronics and computers, they are at least proceeding from a solid foundation. When they expect comparably radical progress in land vehicles, ships, aircraft, rockets, explosives, and energy sources — as many do, either explicitly or implicitly — they are probably mistaken, at least in the early years of the twenty-first century.

A survey that I carried out in 1998 and 1999 suggested that progress in these latter areas of technology is, and will likely remain, modest in the years ahead. As such, the case for aggressively modernizing electronics, munitions, sensors, and communications systems is much more compelling than that for replacing the main vehicles and large weaponry of the armed forces.

The Recent Lessons of the Recent War in Iraq

It is of particular interest to evaluate the RMA hypothesis in light of the recent experience to overthrow Saddam Hussein. Did the war in Iraq, which continues in a different form to this day, validate a new theory of warfare in which special forces, high technology, and creative war plans will replace America's traditional assets of firepower, maneuverability, and brute strength? Some say yes, and now expect U.S. Secretary of Defense Donald Rumsfeld to push for the radical overhaul or "transformation" of the U.S. armed forces that he reportedly wanted back in early 2001 but felt politically unable to pursue. Although different defense scholars hold different views, most expect Rumsfeld to make deep cuts in Army forces in order to fund greater capabilities in airpower, naval forces, missile defenses, space weapons, and special forces.

However, what is most striking about the recent war to overthrow Saddam is just how much traditional combat capabilities have still mattered. This is obvious for the post-invasion, counterinsurgency phase of the mission, now nearly two years old, in which classic infantry tactics, policing skills, and human intelligence operations have been central. But it is also true for the invasion itself.

Yes, special forces and modern airpower were important, but so were Abrams tanks, five-ton supply trucks, rifle-wielding soldiers and Marines, and old-fashioned infantry combat skills. When U.S. forces first faced Hussein's Medina and Baghdad Republican Guard divisions south of the Iraqi capital, they did so with numerical superiority, dominant air support, and tremendous firepower. The recent wars in Afghanistan and Iraq have essentially been won with the military the George W. Bush administration inherited from Bill Clinton, George H.W. Bush, and Ronald Reagan, not with a reinvented force built by proponents of defense revolution. As such, those who would jettison Colin Powell's doctrine of overwhelming force in favor of a Rumsfeld doctrine of stealth, surprise, and finesse should temper their views.

All defense strategists know not to assume that the next war will be like the last one, or to overlearn the lessons of one conflict in anticipation of subsequent military operations. That said, wars are hugely informative events for the discipline of military analysis, and must be mined fully for information and insights whenever they occur. In addition, this particular war is reshaping the basic strategic context of the Persian Gulf region. In particular, it raises questions about the U.S. two-war requirement, which has formed the basis for force planning for over a decade, and about the normal overseas deployments of American forces. For these reasons, it is appropriate to review the war's basic lessons and then suggest preliminary thoughts on their significance for future American defense planning. On balance, they argue for a less radical realignment of the U.S. military than observers have often alleged in the war's immediate aftermath. But changes do not have to be radical to be important, or difficult to get right.

American, British, and Australian forces accomplished a remarkable feat between March 19 and April 9, 2003, the rough boundaries of the main combat phase of military operations in Iraq. They defeated a four-hundred-thousand-man military, overthrew a dictator, and successfully prosecuted major urban combat operations while suffering fewer than two hundred combat losses—even less than in the Persian Gulf War of 1991.

What was responsible for this remarkable battlefield success? In particular, were U.S. Vice President Dick Cheney and Chairman of the Joint Chiefs of Staff Richard Myers right when they claimed that the strategy devised by General Tommy Franks and his colleagues at U.S. Central Command (CENTCOM) was brilliant? Will war colleges around the world be teaching it to their students decades from now? Or will the conflict tend to be seen primarily as a case of overwhelming military capability prevailing over a mediocre army from a mid-sized developing country?

Whether the war's concept deserves to be called brilliant, as some claimed during and right after the war, is debatable. On balance, the U.S. military's performance has been so good and its supremacy so overwhelming that the U.S. probably could have won this war without a brilliant, or even a very good, war plan. That said, there have been major elements of military creativity in the Iraq campaign as well as some that were not new at all.

Consider several key elements:

SHOCK AND AWE. This was of course the bumper sticker for how the war would begin, well advertised weeks in advance. But advertising such an idea tends to reduce its psychological impact. In addition, selectively hitting military targets while sparing civilian infrastructure is an idea that builds on the U.S. experience in Afghanistan, Kosovo, and the Persian Gulf War of 1991. Avoiding attacks against regular Iraqi military units was smart, but it was well-known that these forces were much less loyal to Hussein than were the Special Republican Guard, Republican Guard, and Fedayeen units. Striking hard in a war's early hours is a strategy that air power proponents have counseled for decades. In the end, the shock-and-awe concept was not really followed, because plans apparently changed with the attempt to kill Hussein on March 19, 2003. Even so, given the degree to which Iraqi forces had become accustomed to coalition bombing in the preceding decade, there probably would not have been much shock or awe.

SPECIAL OPERATIONS RAIDS. These were more impressive than the early air campaign. Dozens of small special operations teams disrupted Iraqi command and control, seized oil infrastructure, prevented dams from being demolished, and took hold of airfields in regions where Scud missiles might have been launched at Israel. Special operations and intelligence units also provided information on the whereabouts of Iraqi leaders, permitting the attacks against Hussein and the notorious General Ali Hassan al-Majid, known as "Chemical Ali." They also appear to have disrupted Iraqi lines of communication in Baghdad and elsewhere, perhaps hastening the collapse of Iraqi forces once the urban fights began. These operations were brave, creative, and effective. They also prevented some nightmare scenarios.

BYPASSING SOUTHEASTERN CITIES WHILE RUSHING TO BAGHDAD. In the war's first ten days, it was not clear that the U.S. military could sufficiently protect its flanks in areas that it preferred not to seize. The ensuing debate was a bit hyped; in a worst case, the U.S. could have waited a couple of weeks for other units to arrive with little harm done to the broader strategy. Regardless, this approach, which placed a premium on speed and deep penetration, was not so new. German generals did not make pit stops in Strasbourg or Luxembourg or northeastern France; they homed in directly on Paris.

STRIKING IRAQI FORCES WITH PREPARATORY AIR BOMBARDMENT. The combination of GPS-guided all-weather bombs, better all-weather sensors such as JSTARS aircraft flying well within Iraqi airspace, and real-time joint communications networks denied Iraqi forces any sanctuary. Even if the Iraqis tried to move during sandstorms, or at night, coalition forces could see and strike them. In addition, due to the rapid movements of coalition ground forces, any Iraqi redeployments had to happen quickly if they were to help front-line forces under attack. That made it more likely they would move in large formations on roadways, and they were badly hurt as a result. Again, this was textbook doctrine, applied with devastating effectiveness, rather than brilliant generalship.

DECIMATING COMBINED-ARMS ATTACKS AGAINST THE REPUBLICAN GUARD. In addition to the above combat dynamics, coalition forces were remarkably effective when air and ground units worked together. By the last days of March and early days of April, U.S. forces were severely damaging Republican Guard forces deployed outside of Baghdad. Hussein made a major mistake in keeping them there, perhaps out of fear that they would turn against him if allowed into Baghdad or perhaps out of overconfidence that they could hide in the complex terrain of the Tigris-Euphrates Valley. There were some good tactics on the part of the coalition, such as the U.S. Army's 3rd Mechanized Infantry Division's "bump and run" move to outflank part of the Republican Guard's Medina Division near Karbala. But what won that fight was a devastating display of combined-arms warfare. It built on a decades-old concept with dramatically improved technology that was acquired and integrated into American military doctrine and tactics during the Reagan, George H.W. Bush, and Clinton years. It was less brilliance than sheer dominance.

THE FIGHTS FOR BAGHDAD AND BASRA. Here, there was some genuine cleverness and creativity. To try to seize the cities quickly probably would have produced high casualties on all sides. By contrast, to wait patiently for the U.S. Army's 4th Mechanized Infantry Division and other reinforcements would have given Hussein's forces confidence as well as time to regroup and devise new tactics. So the middle ground — using increasingly assertive "reconnaissance in force" operations to gain information, disrupt Hussein's forces, embolden the Iraqi population to resist, and engage selectively in firefights against elite Iraqi forces — was just right.

On balance, upon reviewing the main pillars of the coalition's success in Iraq, new technology and traditional skills provided a remarkable pair of capabilities. In terms of equipment, of particular note were the all-weather reconnaissance systems, all-weather bombs, and modern communications networks developed in the last decade. (This was during a period when, ironically, advocates of defense revolution were often frustrated at the pace of change in the U.S. armed forces.) In addition, one is struck by the competence of the troops and their commanders, and the excellence of their doctrine and training. Indeed, old-fashioned tanks and urban combat operations performed extremely well.

Implications for the Asia-Pacific Region

With all that as backdrop, I will offer some brief provocations on the implications of this analysis for the Asia-Pacific region.

- U.S. forces in South Korea can now provide as much lethality as before at lower force levels. Cuts of ten to thirty percent, should they be made in the near future, would still leave us stronger than ten to fifteen years ago. As such, the Global Posture Review unveiled in large part in August 2004, which envisions a reduction in American military strength on the peninsula from roughly thirty-seven thousand to twenty-five thousand uniformed personnel, is acceptable.

- Repositioning U.S. forces in South Korea as Secretary Rumsfeld envisions is feasible, and in fact desirable militarily (and economically, given the value of land in Seoul). But the reason has at least as much to do with a stronger South Korean military and a weaker North Korean military than with any military revolution or transformation.

- U.S. forces in Japan can similarly be reconfigured. But again, high technology and new warfighting concepts are only two of the factors. To take the example of the Marines in Okinawa, there are also ways to use greater prepositioning of equipment to achieve equal (or greater) deployable combat capability with fewer forces permanently stationed in the western Pacific region. These concepts rely more on smart use of old-fashioned logistics and transportation assets than on high technology or revolutionary capabilities.

- Even if some opportunities exist for reducing force levels and streamlining the American military footprint abroad, a network of overseas bases is still very important for the U.S. military and nothing about military transformation will change that. The U.S. still needs a number of airfields in any major geographic region to allow for global reach with airlifters, refuelers, and bombers — and also for short-range tactical combat jets to be able to operate intensively in various possible war scenarios. The U.S. still needs places to deploy forces so they can train intensively with allies abroad in places where they might have to fight, and it still needs places to station equipment and supplies to permit rapid reaction in times of crisis.

- U.S. allies are indeed in some danger of falling further behind the United States, given trends in technology and transformation. But that is not inevitable. Note that the U.S. Marine Corps, with its modest budget of about $15 billion a year, manages to keep up with the other U.S. services reasonably well (witness the recent war in Iraq). A similar statement can be made about the United Kingdom's military. These cases suggest that East Asian allies can keep up too, if they make careful and smart choices about how to allocate their defense resources. In fact, South Korea in particular has done an impressive job of making good progress with modest military resources in recent times.

- Missile defense is progressing, but rather slowly, and no complete solutions are on the horizon for addressing the short-range, medium-range, and long-range ballistic missile threats. Still, increasing amounts of partial protection could be available to the U.S. and its allies within a reasonably short time.

[1] For an argument in favor of taking a large part of the active force structure 'off line' so as to devote it to experimentation and acceleration of the RMA, see James R. Blaker, "The American RMA Force: An Alternative to the QDR," *Strategic Review* 25:3, Summer 1997, pp.21-30; for a similar but more general argument, see also Richard K. Betts, *Military Readiness: Concepts, Choices, Consequences*, Brookings Institution Press, Washington, D.C., 1995, pp.35-84. For the view of a conservative critic of the RMA concept, see Frederick W. Kagan, "Wishful Thinking on War," *Weekly Standard*, 15 December 1997, pp.27-29. Kagan argues that the country may need to spend more on technology — but must not do so at the expense of its present engagement and deterrence strategies.

[2] See, most notably, Admiral William A. Owens with Ed Offley, *Lifting the Fog of War*, Farrar, Straus, and Giroux, New York, 2000.

[3] Lawrence Freedman, *The Revolution in Strategic Affairs*, Adelphi Paper 318, Oxford University Press, New York, 1998, p.21.

[4] Martin Van Creveld, *Technology and War: From 2000 B.C. to the Present*, The Free Press, New York, 1989. Trevor Dupuy uses yet another categorization scheme, different from those of Krepinevich, Van Creveld, and others, to understand the history of military innovation. He groups all progress since 1800 together under the title of "the age of technological change." See Trevor N. Dupuy, *The Evolution of Weapons and Warfare*, HERO Books, Fairfax, VA, 1984.

[5] John Keegan, *The First World War*, Alfred A. Knopf, New York, 1999, p.20; Dan Goure, "Is There a Military-Technical Revolution in America's Future?," *Washington Quarterly*, Autumn 1993, p.185; and Dupuy, *The Evolution of Weapons and Warfare*, pp.218-220, 258-266.

[6] Robert Pape, *Bombing to Win: Air Power and Coercion in War*, Cornell University Press, Ithaca, NY, 1996, pp.87-136, 254-313; and Brian Bond and Williamson Murray, "British Armed Forces, 1918-1939," in Allan R. Millet and Williamson Murray, eds., *Military Effectiveness*, vol. II, Unwin Hyman, Boston, 1988.

[7] Stephen Biddle, "Assessing Theories of Future Warfare," Paper Presented to the 1997 Annual Meeting of the American Political Science Association, Washington, D.C., August 1997, pp.37-38; Andrew J. Bacevich, *The Pentomic Era: The U.S. Army between Korea and Vietnam*, National Defense University Press, Washington, D.C., 1986; John Keegan, *A History of Warfare*, Vintage Books, New York, 1993, pp.362-379; Van Creveld, *Technology and War*, pp.193-195; and Stephen Peter Rosen, *Winning the Next War: Innovation and the Modern Military*, Cornell University Press, Ithaca, NY, 1991, pp.13-18, 37-38.

[8] Rosen, *Winning the Next War*, p.252.

[9] National Defense Panel, *Transforming Defense*, pp.7-8.

U.S. Military Strategies and the Korean Peninsula

Koji Murata
Doshisha University

Preface

his paper examines how changes in U.S. military strategies under the George W. Bush administration, particularly since the terrorist attacks of September 11, 2001, can affect situations on the Korean Peninsula and the U.S.-Japan Security Alliance.

I would first like to give an overview of the Bush administration's military strategy. This will be followed by an analysis of the international situation surrounding the Korean Peninsula as well as the domestic political scenes of the countries involved. Finally, I shall attempt to make some policy recommendations in light of the turbulence on the Korean Peninsula and the relative stagnation of issues affecting Okinawa.

Bush Administration Military Strategies

President Bush used the term "balance of power" in his inaugural address in January 2001, echoing Theodore Roosevelt who was fond of using this phrase precisely a century earlier. Inspired by the big naval policy advocated by Admiral Alfred Thayer Mahan, Roosevelt embarked on the expansion of the U.S. Navy and extended the territory covered by the country's security arrangements. Likewise, President Bush had plans to expand the area of national security, including outer space, at the threshold of the new century.

The Bush administration sought to develop and boost U.S. military supremacy through a revolution in military affairs (RMA). More specifically, the president has been promoting the missile defense (MD) initiative, which combines national missile defense (NMD) and theater missile defense (TMD).

The Bush administration's policies towards Asia differed greatly from those pursued by the Clinton administration. President Bush viewed China as a "strategic rival" and took a tougher stance with North Korea, calling on the communist state to engage in comprehensive talks and reduce conventional weapons stockpiles. In contrast, he clearly stressed the importance of the alliance with Japan. It is no accident that many diplomats and national security experts who were behind the U.S.-Japan Security Alliance during the Ronald Reagan and George H.W. Bush presidencies have been appointed to key posts in the current administration. To this extent, Bush foreign policy has been termed "Anything But Clinton."

It was against this backdrop that the Bush administration faced the 9/11 terrorist attacks on New York and Washington. The political center of the U.S. mainland had never been attacked by external forces, except by the British in the War of 1812. The Japanese surprise attack on the Pearl Harbor in 1941 was not against the mainland let alone the capital. Following the assault, the Bush administration declared war against terrorism, stressed the importance of national defense, and sought to establish international cooperation in its efforts to combat terrorism. The U.S. also moved to significantly improve its relations with Russia and China. Japan, as an ally, expeditiously enacted the Anti-Terrorism Special Measures Law in an effort to demonstrate its cooperation with the U.S. North Korea, in contrast, missed an opportunity for dialogue with Washington.

The Bush administration revealed measures aimed to cope with an "asymmetrical threat," such as terrorism, in the U.S. Defense Department's *Quadrennial Defense Review Report* (QDR) published on September 30, 2001. The publication also hinted at China's growing importance, pointing out that "the East Asian littoral — from the Bay of Bengal to the Sea of Japan — represents a particularly challenging area" and that "the possibility exists that a military competitor with a formidable resource base will emerge in the region."[1] The QDR emphasized a need for a superior RMA in a bid to maintain U.S. hegemony on the balance of power between major powers, a two-tier strategy pursued by past administrations.

Reflecting such principles, defense outlays announced the following February jumped by 14.5% from a year earlier to $379 billion. Defense spending by the U.S. alone now accounts for 40% of total global defense expenditure.

For now, however, U.S.-China relations are basically stable, bilateral trade frictions notwithstanding, because of the U.S. expectation that China will play an intermediary role in the Six Party Talks concerning

North Korea's nuclear development. This relationship is also stabilized by America's need to avoid friction with a permanent member of the United Nations Security Council over Iraqi problems, which are addressed below.

President Bush linked Iraq, Iran, and North Korea in an "Axis of Evil" in his State of the Union Address in January 2002, when the military campaign in Afghanistan was practically completed. In particular, he sternly warned Iraq against its alleged plans to develop weapons of mass destruction (WMD), as the possibility of Saddam Hussein's regime developing WMD had been a major concern since the Persian Gulf War of 1991.

When national opinion coalesced behind the president in the aftermath of the terrorist attacks, the time was ripe for the U.S. to resolve the issue once and for all. The question for the Bush administration was not so much "why now" as "why Iraq had not been dealt with earlier." Saddam Hussein had managed to avoid military sanctions against Iraq's alleged development and possession of WMD by intentionally creating ambiguous situations, while continuing to suppress anti-government forces in Iraq and in neighboring countries. As long as WMD are basically political and psychological weapons, strategic ambiguity can be said to have proved quite effective.

Although rumors that the U.S. was prepared to go to war with Iraq unilaterally were circulating, President Bush called on the United Nations to adopt a new resolution on Iraq in September 2002, in a gesture designed to stress his preference for international cooperation in dealing with the country.

The U.S. National Security Strategy published soon afterwards declared, however, that the U.S. "will not hesitate to act alone, if necessary, to exercise our right of self-defense by acting pre-emptively against such terrorists, to prevent them from doing harm against our people and our country."[2] John Gaddis, a diplomatic historian, praises the so-called "Bush Doctrine" as historically important in that it marks departure from policies of "deterrence" and "containment."[3]

The U.S. agreed to a short extension of weapons inspections in Iraq in the face of opposition to military strikes on Iraq from France, Germany, and other countries. At the same time, the U.S. deployed more than two hundred thousand troops to the Persian Gulf and sought to win international endorsement on the use of military power. With the United Nations having failed to adopt a new resolution to replace UN Security Council Resolution 1441, the U.S. issued an ultimatum to Iraq and launched military strikes on the country on March 19, 2003.

Despite earlier predictions for a fierce resistance, the U.S. emerged victorious after a brief campaign, demonstrating anew its military supremacy to the world. Now no "rogue" nation will wish to become a second Iraq by openly antagonizing the U.S. North Korea, for instance, has agreed to participate in three-nation talks with the U.S. and China. The overwhelming victory of the U.S. has apparently helped maintain international order.

The war in Iraq highlighted differences, however, in policy intentions and military capabilities between the U.S. and its allies. The Bush administration prefers to form an alliance of like-minded states to meet changing needs of the day rather than being constrained by the existing framework of allies.

Meanwhile, the Bush administration is increasingly under fire both at home and abroad, partly due to its failure to find weapons of mass destruction in Iraq and partly due to continued strong resistance to the occupation of Iraq. As of the end of 2003, thirty-seven countries have sent personnel to Iraq to assist in post-conflict reconstruction. Japan finally decided in December 2003 to dispatch its Self-Defense Forces after enacting in July 2003 the Law Concerning the Special Measures on Humanitarian and Reconstruction Assistance in Iraq, and having emotionally overcome the loss of the two Japanese diplomats killed in Iraq. The UN Security Council Resolution 1511 approved a U.S. and British-led Coalition Provisional Authority. However, the extent to which the UN can be involved in rehabilitating and stabilizing Iraq depends largely on how much security can be guaranteed to its personnel.

It is indeed ironic that the Bush administration; which had in the past committed itself exclusively to Western alliances such as NATO, the U.S.-Japan Security Alliance, and the U.S.-South Korea alliance, called China a strategic rival, and refused to take part in the tasks of nation-building and peacekeeping; suffers today from increasing friction with its main allies in Western Europe, asserts the importance of the coalition of the like-minded, and passionately tries to improve relations with China — and furthermore, has deployed approximately one-half of the U.S. Army in Iraq and Afghanistan. With anti-terrorist military operations taking place simultaneously on a global scale, the U.S. forces are "stretched to the limit" throughout the world.[4]

Impact on the Korean Peninsula—
International Situation and Domestic Politics

As the international situation surrounding Iraq turns critical, there is increasing ambiguity over the future of the U.S. alliance with South Korea that is pitted against North Korea, another "rogue state."

Anti-U.S. demonstrations reached an unprecedented level in South Korea following the deaths of two junior high school girls hit by a U.S.

armored vehicle in June 2002, and the subsequent acquittal by court-martial of the soldiers involved. Rising South Korean nationalism following the successful co-hosting of soccer's 2002 FIFA World Cup Korea/Japan, a widening gap between the Bush administration's hard-line stance against North Korea and South Korea's Sunshine Policy adopted by former President Kim Dae-jung, and the election of President Roh Moo-hyun in light of growing anti-U.S. sentiment also strained the relationship.

Incidentally, South Korea's Northern Policy, the precursor of the Sunshine Policy, was modeled on the Eastern Policy pursued by the former West Germany. The problem, however, is that the South Korean government pressed ahead with the Northern Policy and subsequent Sunshine Policy without achieving reconciliation with Japan, in contrast to the Eastern Policy, which was based on Germany's reconciliation with France. Of course, the Japanese side must sufficiently account for its part in the impasse.

South Korean perceptions of the strategic importance of U.S. troops stationed in South Korea are changing rapidly. South Korea no longer regards North Korea as its archenemy. Although the U.S. agreed to rectify some of the inequalities imposed on South Korea in the bilateral Status of Forces Agreement (SOFA), public opinion in South Korea remains strongly opposed to U.S. troops in the country, prompting the Bush administration to consider moving U.S. military bases currently located north of Seoul to another region.

U.S. forces in Seoul have functioned as a "fuse" or a "hostage" to protect the capital from possible attacks as North Korea cannot strike Seoul without attacking U.S. forces as well. If the U.S. base were transferred elsewhere and U.S. troops cease to perform the "hostage" role, Seoul may become directly exposed to a threat from North Korean troops.

As early as December 2002, the U.S. and South Korean governments had agreed upon and signed the Future of the Alliance Policy Initiative at the 34th Security Consultative Meeting. In February 2003, U.S. Secretary of Defense Donald Rumsfeld expressed his support for the realignment of U.S. troops in South Korea, saying that it was desirable that part of the ground forces leave Seoul and the demilitarized zone in favor of a naval and air power-centered deployment.[5] This was meant to prevent the Roh government from being swayed by anti-American sentiments. It was also an indication that the U.S. wished to have a highly mobile sea and air force in South Korea deployable out of the region, as required for U.S. worldwide national defense strategies, but also maintain a balanced force including adequate ground forces.

Also, at a U.S.-South Korea summit meeting in May 2003, leaders vowed to revamp their military forces by utilizing new technology and, as they increase their capacity to deal with emerging threats, to work closely together in efforts to modernize their alliance.

In the long run, these trends may be seen as a revival of the phased withdrawal of U.S. forces in South Korea as spelled out in the 1990 East Asia Strategic Initiative.[6] Joint research published in 1994 by the Korea Institute for Defense Analyses and the Rand Corporation in the U.S. discussed the possibility of change in the U.S.-Korea alliance. In the event of a reduced military threat from North Korea, U.S. forces would be rapidly redeployed. And, following the reunification of North and South Korea, the alliance would further evolve into a regional alliance enabling it to contribute to security outside the Korean Peninsula.[7] The North Korean military threat has not been reduced, however, and furthermore it has become unfeasible to deploy an additional 690,000 men in the event of an emergency as contemplated earlier. This means that we must look to the RMA for much of the expected realignment of U.S. forces in South Korea. In fact, the combined command, control, communication, computer, information, monitoring, and surveillance capabilities of the U.S. forces in South Korea have been enhanced in collaboration with the U.S. forces in Japan.

U.S. troop reduction in South Korea may improve the mobility of U.S. forces deployed overseas. (During the war in Iraq, the U.S. forces in South Korea did not leave the country at all.) Some believe that the revival of flexible deployment of forces in South Korea would enhance the ability to dispatch forces overseas and connect U.S. troops in South Korea with the global network of U.S. forces. On the other hand, others point out that by abandoning the trip-wire type of fixed defense, it sends a message to North Korea that even without an attack from Pyongyang, U.S. forces in South Korea could mount an Iraq war-type pre-emptive attack against the North, a situation as good as killing two birds with one stone.[8]

The following are the reported moves of U.S. forces to be effected under the Korea realignment plan:

- ■ The 8th Army Command to move to the rear from Seoul Yongsan to the vicinity of Daejeon;

- ■ The 34th Regional Support Forces to move to the rear from Seoul Yongsan to the vicinity of Daejeon;

- ■ The 1st Communication Brigade to move to the rear from Seoul Yongsan to the vicinity of Daejeon;

- ■ The 2nd Infantry Brigade, 501st Army Corps Support Forces, to move from Uijeongbu to the vicinity of Daejeon;

- ■ The 1st and 2nd Brigades located in Dongducheon to move to the vicinity of Daejeon, and one brigade to withdraw completely by 2006;

- The 7th Air Force, 51st Fighter Company at Osan to maintain the status quo;

- The 6th Calvary Brigade, 23rd Regional Support Corps at Pyontek, to maintain the status quo;

- The 8th Fighter Corps at Kunsan to be withdrawn by 2006;

- The Materials Support Center at Woe-kwan to maintain the status quo;

- The 19th Regional Support Command at Taegum to maintain the status quo;

- The 20th Regional Support Corps at Taegum to maintain the status quo.[9]

The outline of this realignment plan, however, was not made public as originally scheduled in September or October 2003. Nor was the announcement made during Secretary Rumsfeld's visit to Korea in November of that year. It may just be that there is a persistent difference of view between the military leaders in South Korea and Rumsfeld's people in the Pentagon who remain hopeful of promoting the RMA.

In the past, Presidents Richard Nixon and Jimmy Carter announced plans to either reduce U.S. forces stationed in South Korea or pull some of the troops out. The proposed move was partly designed to curb military spending and partly in response to changes in the U.S. assessment of the military threat posed by North Korea. On both occasions, the South Korean government and the general public were united in dissuading the U.S. from carrying out the plan. Ongoing changes in South Korean public opinion regarding the North Korean threat and resentment toward U.S. troops may lead South Korea to encourage the U.S. government to diminish its military presence.[10]

In view of the gravity of the situation, President Roh is mounting efforts to improve South Korea's relationship with the U.S. South Korea is now afraid of being deserted by the U.S. as well as being drawn into war as a result of the U.S. military's move to the rear and its possible pre-emptive strike on North Korea with high-tech weapons. Washington, however, remains indifferent to efforts being made by Seoul. President Roh, for his part, is having difficulties containing the anti-U.S. camp, which constitutes a major domestic support base for his administration.

According to a survey in July 2002, forty-four percent of the respondents indicated that they had a negative view of the U.S., while this figure climbed to fifty-one percent for the eighteen to twenty-nine-year-old group. In a further survey conducted in May 2003, however, the overall ratio increased to fifty percent, while for the eighteen to twenty-nine-year-old group it rose dramatically to seventy-one percent.

Furthermore, fifty-five percent of the participants in the May 2003 survey indicated that pre-emptive strikes could not be justified. In addition, only twenty-eight percent of the respondents in South Korea believed North Korea was a great danger to regional security compared to thirty-eight percent in the U.S., showing a significant disparity.[11]

Moreover, President Roh's domestic political foundation is extremely vulnerable. For the first time in the history of South Korean constitutional government, the president was forced in December 2003 to concede to a referendum challenging the nation's confidence in his leadership. Due to political scandals involving the opposition party, however, the referendum was not implemented. Despite continued accusations by the opposition party, Roh's party was somehow able to win the only general election to be held under his government in April 2004.

South Korea has already dispatched a seven-hundred-member non-combatant unit to Iraq, and its offer to Secretary Rumsfeld to send an additional eight thousand men was received coolly. The deaths of two South Korean civilians in Iraq at the end of November 2004 will likely increase anti-American public opinion concerning South Korea's cooperation with the United States. (In this regard, the South Korean government's position vis-à-vis U.S. cooperation is similar to that during the Vietnam War.)

In June 2004, the U.S. announced that it will reduce the number of U.S. military personnel in South Korea by one-third (twelve thousand troops) by December 2005. Though South Korea has strengthened its ability to defend itself, it is in intense negotiations to postpone the reduction. In August 2004, President Bush stated that the U.S. will reduce the number of troops stationed overseas by sixty to seventy thousand over the next ten years. Thus, reduction in the number of U.S. troops in South Korea and realignment of the U.S. troops in Japan might include even greater numbers.

The Okinawa Connection

In the worst-case scenario, if U.S. troop strength in South Korea is sharply reduced, Japan may well become the front line of U.S. forward deployment in East Asia against possible military threats from North Korea and China's growing military presence. Japan may be forced to play a part similar to that played by former West Germany as the front line against the armed forces of the former Soviet Union during the Cold War, or that played by South Korea until now against North Korea across the thirty-eighth parallel. Robyn Lim calls Japan a "new South Korea" under this scenario.[12]

In any event, Japan, the United States, and South Korea have yet to coordinate their policies, as the three countries differ in their perceptions of the North Korean threat in terms of conventional weapons and nuclear arms. For instance, some Japanese were skeptical of the effectiveness of "the American nuclear umbrella" as a deterrent against North Korea's alleged development of nuclear arms and called for nuclear armament of Japan. This may be an overreaction, however, since even during the Cold War when U.S.-European relations were troubled by the proposition of strategic nuclear coupling (the question as to whether the U.S. would go to the defense of Paris and London at the risk of sacrificing New York and Chicago), the two sides maintained a policy of deterrence.

The alliance between the U.S. and South Korea is not the only one facing a crisis. France and Germany were strongly opposed to the U.S. and British-led war on Iraq. Scholar Francis Fukuyama, famous for predicting "the end of history," is now predicting the end of alliances formed in the aftermath of World War II.[13] If the U.S.-South Korean alliance or NATO falls into disarray, it will become all the more important to maintain and reinforce the U.S.-Japan Security Alliance. (The so-called neo-conservatives in the U.S. are showing a more lenient attitude towards a cooperative Japan in contrast to the defiant countries of Europe. Their ignorance of Japan is also a factor affecting their perceptions.)

In particular, bases for aircraft carriers will assume greater importance for flexible forward deployment. The U.S. Air Force's Kadena Air Base in Okinawa Prefecture is also likely to play a more significant role in terms of securing command of the air and maintaining a strategic balance in the Taiwan Strait in the event of an emergency in the Korean Peninsula. It will also play a role in countering the modernization of China's missiles. The largest U.S. air base in the Pacific, Kadena possesses forty-eight F-15 fighters, ten HH-60s for combat search and rescue, fifteen KC-135 air-refueling tankers, and two E-3s with airborne warning and control systems (AWACS). In any event, Okinawa is closer to Pyongyang than Tokyo. The U.S. forces in Okinawa may be the ideal model of force mix for future deployments. Secretary Rumsfeld's visit to Okinawa in November 2003 was the first in thirteen years by a U.S. secretary of defense. The discussion between the secretary and Okinawa Governor Inamine, who demanded a drastic revision of the Okinawa base agreement, moved along parallel tracks.[14]

Moreover, the U.S. government has come under fire even in Japan over the war in Iraq. Many Japanese are concerned that the allied forces have failed to discover weapons of mass destruction. A majority were against the December 2003 decision to dispatch the Self-Defense Forces (SDF) to Iraq. According to the *Asahi Shimbun* on December 12, 2003, fifty-five percent were opposed while thirty-four percent supported the move, and the government support ratio fell to forty-one percent from the forty-seven percent it registered in the previous poll in November (since then, however, support for the SDF deployment has been increasing).

Under these circumstances, if U.S. forces are consolidated in South Korea, the Japanese public is likely to pressure the U.S. government to do the same in Japan. In particular, if deployment outside the region becomes possible for the U.S. forces in South Korea, reduction of the U.S. Marine Corps in Okinawa may be discussed. Already in March 2001, the governments of the U.S. and South Korea agreed to a Land Partnership Plan, which stipulates that land used by the U.S. forces will be reduced from 244.2 million square meters to about 45 million square meters and the main facilities, including three training grounds, will be reduced from the present forty-one locations to twenty-three. In other words, the U.S. forces will be returning to South Korea sixty-eight percent of the facilities and fifty-five percent of the land. The total cost of the moves is estimated to be approximately $500 million. This represents a far greater scheme for consolidation and integration than any contemplated for Okinawa. While there may not be a large-scale reduction of U.S. troops in South Korea for now, the consolidation of bases and facilities is progressing quietly.

Revision of the U.S.-Japan SOFA is especially controversial. Central to the issue is Article 17.5 of the agreement. A revision of its provisions would affect the criminal trial system in Japan and have an impact on similar accords between the U.S. and other nations (Japan is but one of the forty allies of the U.S.).

At present, the SOFA dictates that custody transfers of individuals accused of matters over which the host country has primary jurisdiction occur after indictment by the host country. After an agreement was reached in October 1995 by a joint committee concerned with criminal court proceedings, however, in murder, rape, and other specific cases, the accused may be handed over even before indictment. NATO's SOFA, by contrast, still stipulates custody transfer after indictment, while the U.S.-Korea SOFA calls for transfer when a judicial ruling by the host country is made and enforced — which is limited to twelve types of crimes (specifics unknown) — with the codicil that transfer may be possible after an indictment. Likewise, the Bonn Supplementary Agreement stipulates transfer when a judicial ruling is made and enforced. In actuality, Germany has in almost all cases surrendered the right to primary jurisdiction. One can say, at least formally and on this particular issue, the U.S.-Japan SOFA is favorable to the Japanese side.

Nevertheless, crime is on the increase in Okinawa. According to the Okinawa Prefectural Police, there were eighty-one criminal arrests of U.S. military personnel, civilian Army employees, and their families involving one hundred persons in 2002, the fourth consecutive year the number increased. Considering Okinawan public opinion, the passive argument that amendment of the SOFA is like opening a Pandora's Box no longer seems to hold. Since Japanese police consider confession an important element in making an arrest, the U.S. side demanded that a witness be allowed to attend any police interrogations. At home in Japan, too, this problem came to the fore in the process of judicial reform and there were also movements seeking to secure the rights of victims. In April 2004, to strengthen cooperation during investigations, the U.S.-Japan Joint Committee agreed to allow a representative from the U.S. military to be present during interrogations of U.S. soldiers.[15]

Furthermore, safeguarding the environment as a feature of the SOFA will become even more vital. An environmental impact assessment (started in 2003) for the Henoko coastal district of the city of Nago, a candidate for the relocation of Futenma Air Station, will take at least three years. And, even if construction of the new base proceeds without delays, some say that the project would only be completed at the earliest in 2019.

Major U.S. bases in Japan also function as bases for UN forces. Should the U.S. pledge to maintain the regime in North Korea and the two nations sign a peace treaty, the state of war in the Korean Peninsula would cease and UN forces might leave U.S. bases in Japan. If North Korea poses a renewed military threat, however, Japan, the U.S., and South Korea would need a new legal framework to allow the three nations to coordinate military actions.

The fluidity of Japan's domestic politics is the problem. Having secured a stable majority in the November 2003 general election, the coalition government finds itself in a precarious situation over the dispatch of Self-Defense Forces to Iraq. According to *Asahi Shimbun* polls, the approval rating of the Koizumi government plummeted following the decision to dispatch SDF. If SDF personnel were to die in Iraq, the government's position would become even more precarious.

Plus, in the June 2004 House of Councilors election, the opposition Democratic Party of Japan gained many seats and this will make managing the political agenda more difficult for the Koizumi government. In this political environment, the government will have to address issues that could spark strong reaction from domestic and foreign quarters. These include review of the defense outline, promotion of the Japan Defense Agency to a ministry, and formulating the procedural law for constitutional amendments.

With regard to North Korea, Japan has yet to resolve the abduction issue, and it is increasingly difficult for the government to take a flexible stance before a strong public opinion is formed concerning this issue. The failure in November 2003 to launch a reconnaissance satellite is one more example why Japan must continue to depend on the U.S. for intelligence gathering and other needs involving North Korean security issues, another source of increased public frustration.

A worsening of the situation in Iraq could become an Achilles' heel and require deployment of additional forces, which could create pressure to reduce U.S. ground forces in South Korea. The Bush administration needs international support over the Iraq problem. The degree of cooperation from Japan and South Korea will have a defining impact on their relations with America.

Confusion in post-conflict Iraqi governance appears to have diminished the "neo-conservative" influence on the administration. (Incidentally, I believe that the media in Japan tends to overvalue its influence.) Having noted this, the most powerful political support for the administration comes from the grass-roots religious right wing. An exit poll in the 2000 presidential election noted that fourteen percent of voters identified themselves as "religious right wing," and seventy-nine percent of those voted for Bush.[16] On foreign policy, these voters believe that defense of the homeland is most important — in contrast to the "neo-conservatives" who value active American intervention overseas — but support the use of America's military power around the world for this purpose. These trends among Bush supporters may spur a policy favorable to overseas deployment of U.S. forces and hinder the return of the U.S. to cooperative internationalism, against the wishes of otherwise willing allies such as Japan and South Korea.

Issues and Recommendations

As noted before, the Bush administration is advocating pre-emptive strikes. It is not rare to see the actual course of action taken by the U.S. government differ from its declared foreign policy. The "massive retaliation strategy" adopted by the Dwight Eisenhower administration is a case in point. In this sense, it would be rather dangerous to take the argument for pre-emptive attacks at face value. The war in Iraq of 2003 should be viewed as the final phase of a thirteen-year-long Persian Gulf War, which began in 1991, rather than the initiation of the "Bush Doctrine." Pre-emptive attacks evoke a string of negative notions. It is essential to clearly define the concept to ensure the consistency of military strategies among U.S. allies.

Today, the U.S. is by far the largest military power in the world and the country is psychologically prepared to use its military might. The word "empire" has often been used to describe the U.S. in recent years. This is not just a passing phenomenon under the Bush administration but also one affecting the broad international political structure. Maintaining the U.S.-Japan Security Alliance with such a superpower is becoming an increasingly sensitive task.

At the same time, countries in alliance with such a militarily powerful country might stand to benefit enormously. Have not Japan, South Korea, and Western European countries become somewhat indifferent to this aspect?

Certainly, excessive military intervention by the U.S. is likely to generate resentment and anxiety in the international community. On the other hand, if feelings of isolation cause the U.S. to wash its hands of international affairs and become increasingly insular, it will have a gravely adverse impact.

It is of the utmost importance for Japan, the U.S., and South Korea to coordinate policies to enable the U.S. military to maintain its forward deployment in a stable and flexible manner.

The past two Six Party Talks in Beijing discussing North Korea's nuclear problem did not produce any concrete results. While in one sense this outcome was expected, perhaps it indicated how much North Korea has deepened its isolation in multilateral talks. It may be that it is adopting a wait-and-see attitude on developments in Iraq.

North Korea, however, will often make an about face and eventually will probably return to the negotiation table. That said, the multilateral talks may well require considerable time before a peaceful solution can be reached. To weather negotiations with North Korea, which are likely to be protracted, it is important for Japan, the U.S., and South Korea to show increased sensitivity to the domestic politics of the other two countries. At the same time, it is important to promote dialogue on security issues and strengthen the alliance framework to reduce the possibility of relations among them having a major impact on domestic politics. It is also important to strengthen relations with China as the mediator nation.

Below, I wish to make certain proposals regarding the Okinawa issue in relation to the situation on the Korean Peninsula, particularly with regard to the possibility of the reduction of U.S. troop strength in Korea as well as the consolidation and integration of bases.

Let me begin by making some general points:

(1) Concerning Iraq, South Korea sent a sizable non-combatant unit and Japan dispatched its Self-Defense Forces. Moreover, both countries are standing by their decision regardless of the deaths of their civilians in Iraq at about the same time. (Even despite the two kidnapping incidents of Japanese nationals in April 2004, the Japanese government refuses to withdraw its SDF.) South Korea has also suppressed negative views among its citizens over Japan's

decision to send its forces abroad. Continued positive support by Japan and South Korea, assuming the expansion (in the U.S.) of a policy favoring international cooperation, will provide the essential premise for policy coordination among Japan, South Korea, and the U.S.

(2) There will be greater need in the future for the international community to be actively involved in rebuilding "bankrupt states," in peacekeeping operations (PKOs), and in fighting terrorism. Japan and South Korea together should study ways to enable joint training and operations — involving other states as necessary — to conduct maritime salvage operations, manage piracy, engage in PKOs, develop anti-terrorist measures, and take Proliferation Security Initiatives (PSI) with, for example, North Korea in mind. If the question of collective self-defense becomes an obstacle for Japan to undertake the above initiatives, it should find ways to resolve the issue, pending the final report of the Joint Houses Constitution Research Committee.

(3) Notwithstanding the popular rhetoric about the importance of the U.S.-Japan Security Alliance, its supporting foundations in both countries are not necessarily firm. According to a Japan-U.S. poll conducted jointly by the *Yomiuri Shimbun* and the Gallup Organization, fifty-four percent of Americans think present bilateral relations are good, while only forty-one percent of Japanese agree. In both countries, the percentage has dropped thirteen points since last year. Asked if the other country was trustworthy, seventy-one percent of Americans and forty-one percent of Japanese gave an affirmative answer. Given this changeable reality, Japan in particular should make more efforts to nurture American experts on Japan and develop personal relationships.

Let me now turn to the specifics:

(4) Given the anti-American public opinion in South Korea, strong support in certain American quarters for the RMA, and the shortage of deployable troops overseas; the reduction of U.S. forces in South Korea could materialize. Short of that, U.S. bases in South Korea will probably be consolidated. Without substantial improvement in North Korean relations, these trends will strategically work to increase the importance of the U.S. bases in Okinawa, but at the same time politically strengthen Okinawan demands for the reduction of the U.S. bases. While maintaining the strategic rationale and managing problems caused by the bases in Okinawa, excessive public agitation should be curbed. To that end, implementation of the U.S.-Japan SOFA should be both reviewed and revised. Related to the issue of allowing the presence of a U.S. official during interrogation of an American suspect, as a result

of the latest review of SOFA implementation, Japanese authorities are now allowed to take custody of U.S. military personnel prior to indictment for all crimes. We should continue to pursue review of SOFA implementation and strive for revision in the long term by working to guarantee the human rights of accused individuals within the framework of judicial reform in Japan. Okinawa may not be completely satisfied with this move, but it must take this opportunity to renew interest of the Japanese government and the general public in the Okinawa issue. With regard to the environmental standards to be applied to the U.S. bases, on the other hand, it may be possible to revise the SOFA to accommodate Japanese demands. In any case, the application of the required standards should await revision of the agreement. Insisting that the U.S. take responsibility for the environment before the revision would narrow the margin for compromise. Currently accepted "global standards" should be applied in the areas of human rights and the environment. Compared to these issues, taxing cars owned by American military personnel and employed civilians and their families offer minor advantages, even financially, and would only cause unnecessary psychological disruptions to the far more important bilateral relations.

(5) The completion of an alternative facility to Futenma is expected in 2019 at the earliest, after an environmental assessment is conducted. Then a "fifteen-year limitation" to its use will be applied, which will take us to 2034. It is totally unpractical to predict now what the strategic environment will be then. That is like being able to guess in 1972, when Okinawa was returned to Japan, what the current strategic environment would be like. Turning it the other way around, this arrangement may in fact amount to giving the U.S. Army a free hand at using the bases regardless of the strategic environment. The fifteen-year limit should be redefined as a political expression of the Okinawan people's will rather than as a fixed time schedule. An informal forum should be established for the U.S. administration, the Japanese government, and Okinawa Prefecture to regularly exchange views on the East Asian strategic situation. In order not to abuse the forum by merely airing its grievances, Okinawa should establish a think tank that will address not just its own problems concerning the U.S. bases but the strategic environment of East Asia, and work to expand the intellectual network to include similar think tanks on the main Japanese islands and in the U.S., South Korea, and other countries.

While there is no remedy that would drastically alter the present situation, given the fluidity of the Korean Peninsula and the languid circumstances surrounding Okinawa, we must continue our efforts toward a solution, while carefully tracking big changes in international affairs. It is a classic case of needing to think globally and act locally. Okinawa must catch itself for neglecting the former while the rest of Japan and the U.S. tend to overlook the latter. Neither must be ignored.

---

[1] U.S. Department of Defense, *Quadrennial Defense Review Report,* 30 September 2001, p.4.

[2] *The National Security Strategy of the United States of America,* September 2002, p.6.

[3] John L. Gaddis, "A Grand Strategy of Transformation," *Foreign Policy,* November/December 2002.

[4] Harlan Ullman, "Washington Insider's View," *Sekai Shuho: World Affairs Weekly,* 19-26 August 2003, pp.6-7.

[5] *Washington Post,* 14 February 2003.

[6] U.S. Department of Defense, *A Strategic Framework for the Asian Pacific Rim: Looking toward the 21st Century,* July 1990.

[7] Jonathan D. Pollack, Young Koo Cha, and others, *A New Alliance for the Next Century: The Future of U.S.-Korean Security Cooperation,* RAND, Santa Monica, CA, 1995.

[8] "Tesshu kotai setsu no naka no zaikanbeigun" (U.S. forces in South Korea under rumors of withdrawal and retreat), *Sentaku,* January 2004, p.13.

[9] Ibid., pp.13-14.

[10] Refer to Koji Murata, Daitoryo no zasetsu — kata seiken no zaikanbeigun tettai seisaku (A setback of a president — the Carter administration's policy of withdrawing U.S. forces in Korea), *Yuhi-kaku,* Tokyo, 1998.

[11] *Stars and Stripes,* 28 August 2003.

[12] Robyn Lim, "Japan as the'New South Korea'?" paper submitted to the U.S-Japan-Taiwan Trilateral Dialogue, Tokyo Round, 2-3 March 2003.

[13] Francis Fukuyama, "End of the Postwar Alliance Pact," *Daily Yomiuri,* 16 March 2003.

[14] *Ryukyu Shimpo,* 17 November 2003.

[15] Koji Murata, "Okinawa kuesuchon no kaiketsu wo hakaru tame ni" (Answering the 'Okinawa question'), *Sekai Shuho: World Affairs Weekly,* 27 April 2004, pp.40-41.

[16] *Asahi Shimbun,* 3 December 2003.

U.S.-China Relations and the Implications for Okinawa

Michael D. Swaine
Carnegie Endowment for International Peace

T he Sino-American relationship is arguably the most complex bilateral inter-state relationship in the world. Strong elements of mutual economic dependence and benefit, common regional and global interests, and significant amounts of public admiration and affinity coexist alongside occasionally intense levels of political and ideological friction, emerging great power tensions, and considerable levels of distrust, fear, and antipathy, especially regarding highly sensitive territorial issues such as Taiwan. As a continental Asian power and as a global-spanning maritime power, it is inevitable that much of the strategic interaction between China and the United States is focused on the western Pacific. This is especially the case in the realm of political-military security relations, given, on the one hand, China's historical experience of conflict with Japan and on the Korean Peninsula, its growing concern with the defense of its economically booming eastern coast, and its desire to prevent the emergence of an independent Taiwan, and, on the other hand, America's longstanding desire to maintain both its overall position of military superiority in littoral Asia and the credibility of its longstanding security and political commitments to South Korea, Japan, and Taiwan.

It is thus no surprise that, as a close ally, economic partner, and democratic friend of the United States, as a basing area for critical forward deployed U.S. forces in Asia, and as a close neighbor, competitor, and past historical adversary of China, Japan is deeply affected by the character and evolution of the Sino-American relationship. And, among the islands of the Japanese archipelago, Okinawa is particularly subject to such influence, especially in the security arena. This is due both to its close proximity to Taiwan, the Korean Peninsula, and the southeastern coast of mainland China, and to the fact that the island serves as a basing area for a significant number of U.S. air, naval, and ground forces that possess the capability to operate far beyond the main Japanese islands.

Given the aforementioned historical tensions and disparate interests that exist between China and the United States, one cannot assume that those U.S. forces would not be drawn into a future American confrontation with China over any number of contentious issues involving both countries, from Taiwan and the Korean Peninsula to the Spratly Islands in the South China Sea. Okinawa could thus benefit from — and possibly contribute to — the consolidation of a stable, cooperative, and peaceful Sino-American relationship. On the other hand, it could also be exposed to serious security threats and instability as a result of a highly antagonistic U.S.-China relationship. Moreover, under certain circumstances, military conflict between the two powers could result in devastating consequences for the island.

This paper will first examine the broad context of U.S.-China relations, highlighting both the current strengthened foundation for cooperation that exists between the two countries and the continued presence of factors that could produce confrontation and even conflict in the future. In the latter area, the Taiwan problem is especially significant and thus receives particular attention. The specific implications of the preceding analysis for Okinawa are then examined in some detail, focusing in particular on the potential Chinese threat to the island resulting from the presence of U.S. forces. The final section of the paper will discuss the options available to Okinawa to reduce the potential dangers to which it is exposed by its association with the U.S.-China relationship.

The Good News: A More Cooperative Sino-American Relationship

The prospects for a stable, beneficial and peaceful U.S.-China relationship — over at least the near term — seem to have improved significantly during the past three years. The harsh rhetoric and tense encounters of the early George W. Bush era have given way to growing signs of cooperation between the two nations.[1] Both sides have agreed to downplay or put aside their most potentially volatile differences in order to address common problems, especially the struggle against global terrorism.

This fundamental shift was confirmed on the U.S. side by the Bush administration's National Security Strategy of September 2002. This important policy document identified global terrorism — not a rising China — as America's primary strategic threat, and clearly asserted the need for Washington to work closely with China and other major powers to combat this threat and to ensure global order. On the Chinese side, Beijing has offered significant levels of assistance to Washington in the war against terror and, since fall 2002, greatly strengthened its formal mechanisms for enforcing internal controls over the export of WMD-related or dual-use items from China. As a result of both countries' heightened commitment to greater cooperation, hard-liners in Beijing and Washington have been quieted, at least for the present.

The most significant change behind the current improvement in U.S.-China relations originated in the United States. Prior to the events of September 11, 2001, the Bush administration was largely divided over how to handle China. Vice President Dick Cheney, Secretary of Defense Donald Rumsfeld and their tough-minded subordinates — all proponents of global stability through unqualified U.S. dominance — believed that U.S. policy toward China must focus on actively constraining, if not containing, Beijing. This effort was to be implemented through a multi-faceted policy combining expanding military deployments in and access to Asia with greater political and military assistance to Taiwan, strengthened political relations with democratic allies and friends, and the overall treatment of China as a nascent strategic adversary. Any effort to engage China had to be clearly subordinated to the requirements of these larger policy goals.

In contrast, while supporting many elements of the Rumsfeld-Cheney approach (in particular the need to hedge against potential Chinese aggression over the long term), the U.S. State Department under Secretary of State Colin Powell believed that Washington needed to reduce the intense level of distrust and antagonism between the two countries that had emerged after the highly acrimonious EP-3 incident of April 2001. This perspective recognized that America's enormous and expanding economic and technological involvement with China, Beijing's growing influence in Asia and within important global and regional international organizations, and the fundamentally indeterminate nature of China's future political orientation combined to argue in favor of greater bilateral stability and cooperation in handling a growing number of common problems.

These two approaches to China coexisted for many months within the Bush administration and produced a sometimes erratic, inconsistent public articulation of policy. The events of September 11 significantly increased Washington's need for immediate cooperation with the major powers, however, and deflected attention away from more long-term concerns, such as the rise of China as a peer competitor. As a consequence, the State Department/Powell approach became more compelling, and eventually elicited strong support for improved relations with China not only from President Bush but also from Vice President Cheney.

China's decision to greatly reduce the level of friction with Washington and to cooperate in the war on terror and in other important areas such as nonproliferation greatly facilitated the shift in Washington's stance. The Chinese policy change began well before 9/11, but was greatly stimulated by that tragedy. The Chinese leadership quickly realized that the basic reorientation of American strategy precipitated by the attacks of September 11 presented major advantages and opportunities for China, at least over the short to medium term. September 11 not only overrode or at least muted concerns in the U.S. over the strategic challenge posed by a rising China, it also provided a new foundation for improved relations with Washington in the form of a joint struggle against terrorism. In short, China's leaders recognized early on that 9/11 would provide significant "breathing room" while increasing the value to the U.S. of amicable U.S.-China relations.

Beijing's policy shift also stems from a growing recognition that China's economic attractiveness to Taiwan, as well as its overall domestic stability, are increasingly dependent on deepening trade, investment, and technological links with the U.S. In the past two to three years, the United States has in many ways become the most critical engine for China's continued high rate of economic growth. Antagonistic relations with Washington could damage U.S.-China economic ties, weaken the Chinese economy, and thereby greatly reduce China's magnetic pull on Taiwan. Such a development could also weaken popular support for the Chinese government.

Finally, growing Chinese political and economic influence, both regionally and globally, has diminished China's longstanding insecurities in the international arena. Chinese leaders are more confident in their interactions with other powers, whether on a bilateral or multilateral basis, or via international regimes, and feel they enjoy new, more subtle forms of leverage against potential American pressure. This is particularly evident in China's relations with South Korea and many members of ASEAN. This change has reduced Beijing's past inclination to confront the U.S. openly over a variety of issues.[2]

The Bad News: The Possibility of a Sino-American Confrontation Remains

These positive developments in U.S.-China relations benefit Okinawa by strengthening the overall prospects for peace, stability, and prosperity in the potentially tumultuous western Pacific. One cannot assume, however, that this beneficial environment will continue indefinitely. Although the current marked improvement in U.S.-China relations exhibits some depth and potential durability, the underlying factors driving this transformation do not amount to a fundamental strategic convergence of interests. Washington and Beijing continue to hold different views on many key security issues, from China's future strategic posture in Asia, to some aspects of WMD proliferation, the future of the Korean Peninsula (and the disposition of the current crisis over North Korea's nuclear weapons program), the handling of political developments on Taiwan, the structure of the Asian trade and investment system, and the overall position and role of U.S. power in the Asia-Pacific.[3] Since the Bush administration took office, Beijing has also grown more concerned over heightened U.S. military deployments in the Asia-Pacific, along with the deepening of U.S. political and military ties with Taiwan. And since the events of September 11, the Chinese leadership has also expressed concern over the potential long-term implications of the growing U.S. political and military presence in Central and South Asia.

For its part, the United States continues to hedge significantly against the possible long-term emergence of a strong and assertive China opposed to the existing American presence in Asia. Washington also remains prepared for the possibility of a confrontation over Taiwan and is concerned about other territorial disputes involving China such as the Spratly Islands issue in the South China Sea.[4] Moreover, although quiet for now, hard-liners in both capitals continue to harbor strong suspicions regarding the motives and actions of the other side and advocate policies designed to contain or undermine each state's power or influence.

The Taiwan Issue Remains the Greatest Concern

Many of the above enduring security issues in the Sino-American relationship could exert a significant — and potentially adverse — impact on Okinawa. This is because American forces on the island influence U.S. and Chinese deterrence perceptions and warfighting capabilities in many of the above cases. Among these, the most important is the Taiwan issue.

The island of Taiwan and its surrounding areas have been an irritant in the U.S.-China relationship since the early fifties. A persistent level of Sino-American tension over the island has been and will likely remain unavoidable. This is largely due to the basic contradiction between, on the one hand, the Chinese claim to sovereignty over Taiwan combined with Beijing's refusal to renounce the possible use of force to prevent Taiwanese independence, and, on the other, the strong U.S. commitment to a peaceful solution to the issue, reinforced by U.S. political and diplomatic support for what most Americans view as a longstanding, close friend and, in recent years, a robust democracy. Despite China's claim to sovereignty over the island, the United States is committed to providing Taiwan with the military means to maintain its defensive-oriented deterrence capability against the mainland, to ensuring the freedom from coercion of Taiwan's new democracy, and, more broadly, to maintaining stability across the Taiwan Strait.

Although for the most part highly manageable over the four decades since the communist victory on the mainland, tensions over Taiwan have intensified during the past fifteen years to generate a very real chance of conflict between the two powers. This has occurred largely as a result of the interplay between two major trends occurring on the island and the mainland. On the one hand, the democratization of the political process on the island, bolstered by Taiwan's economic success and growing economic involvement with the international community, have enormously strengthened popular support for a separate Taiwanese political identity and increased popular awareness of the major differences in living standards and political systems between mainland China and Taiwan. On the other hand, a rapid expansion in cross-Strait economic and social ties, along with relatively high levels of Chinese military growth (much of which is now directed toward Taiwan), have created fears of growing Chinese leverage over the island, along with concerns that China might use its expanding military clout to coerce or force Taiwan to accept reunification on Beijing's terms.

These adverse political, economic, and military trends have led to the collapse of the former modus vivendi across the Taiwan Strait that had provided stability for over forty years, centering on a common acceptance by both Beijing and Taipei of the status of Taiwan as part of China and a gradual reduction in the level of military preparedness each side directed toward the other.[5] During the past twelve to fifteen years, this shared belief has been gradually replaced by what is in effect a "one China, one Taiwan" situation that is entirely unacceptable to Beijing, accompanied by strong levels of mutual distrust between the two sides and the gradual emergence of an incipient arms race across the Taiwan Strait. The explosive growth that has occurred over the past five to six years in cross-Strait economic and person-to-person ties has arguably strengthened the belief in some quarters that deepening interdependence will facilitate an eventual resolution of the problem. But more recent actions taken by Taiwan's President Chen Shui-bian — centered on efforts to hold public referenda on the Chinese threat and to enact a new constitution that removes any association with China — have seriously undermined such optimism, at least on the Chinese side.[6]

    In the absence of a new stabilizing modus vivendi across the
Taiwan Strait, peace and stability now rest to a considerable extent
upon the ability of the United States to both deter and reassure Beijing
regarding Taiwan.[7] Specifically, China must be deterred from utilizing
military force to halt or reverse what it views as steady incremental
movement by Taiwan toward independence. And if deterrence fails,
U.S. (and Taiwanese) forces must possess the capability to resolve
any subsequent military conflict on terms favorable to both powers.
At the same time, to maintain stability, China must be reassured that
such superior U.S. and Taiwanese deterrent capabilities will not be
used to shield Taiwan from a Chinese attack as it moves toward formal
independence.[8]

    U.S. forces based in Okinawa would likely play a critical role in
fulfilling the deterrence and, if necessary, the warfighting component of
this strategic calculus toward China. Specialized aircraft deployed from
the U.S. Air Force's Kadena Air Base currently perform surveillance
and reconnaissance duties along the Chinese coast that are essential
to the development of operational plans against vital Chinese military
and political assets. Such plans would be critical to the successful
prosecution of any military action against China during a Taiwan
crisis. Kadena-based aircraft would also augment U.S. efforts to obtain
early warning of a possible Chinese attack against Taiwan. Even more
important, two squadrons of approximately forty to fifty Kadena-based
F-15 fighters, supported by aerial refueling aircraft, would constitute
a vital nearby component of U.S. air power capable of reaching the
Taiwan Strait in a relatively short period of time — i.e., possibly within
hours — after the outbreak of a crisis or conflict between Beijing and
Taipei. The rapid deployment of these U.S. air assets could prove critical
to the success of efforts to deter or defeat a Chinese attack, especially
if such an attack focused on the rapid establishment by China of a fait
accompli requiring air superiority over the Taiwan Strait, e.g., through a
quick, intense aerial bombardment and/or the seizure of key Taiwanese
assets by airborne special forces.[9]

    Fighter aircraft from one or more U.S. carriers and/or fighters and
bombers based in central Japan, Guam, South Korea, or even more
distant locations such as Central Asia, the Middle East, or Hawai'i could
also be deployed in a Taiwan crisis.[10] These aircraft could conceivably
substitute for Okinawa-based aircraft under certain circumstances.
However, the reaction time — and hence the utility — of more distant
aircraft would depend heavily on the extent of early warning time
provided, as well as the existing state of readiness of the aircraft in
question, given the longer distances involved and the consequent need
for extensive mid-air refueling. The availability of such distant aircraft
for missions in the vicinity of Taiwan would also constitute a critical
factor. Many combat aircraft and/or refueling tankers might already be

committed to missions in other regions of the world at the time of a Taiwan crisis. In addition, in order to sustain combat operations over Taiwan, fighter aircraft and bombers would almost certainly need to land somewhere near the island to be rearmed, refueled, and possibly repaired.[11] Kadena Air Base would be the most logical choice for such support activities. Given these complex requirements, one cannot assume that large numbers of land-based aircraft could be deployed from distant locations in a matter of hours — much less sustained in the vicinity of Taiwan — without relying on U.S. bases or forces in Okinawa.[12]

Aside from their use during the potentially critical initial phase of a military crisis over Taiwan, Kadena-based F-15s, AWACs, aerial refueling aircraft, P-3 anti-submarine warfare (ASW) patrol planes, and storage, landing, refueling, and rearming facilities could provide critical support for carrier deployments and long-range, land-based aircraft deployments to the Taiwan area, as well as surveillance, battle damage assessments, and command and control capabilities for both U.S. and Taiwanese forces during any phase of a crisis or conflict. In addition, U.S. bases in Okinawa could offer the essential means for U.S. forces to undertake emergency evacuation of Americans and other foreign nationals during a Taiwan crisis. Such functions could be performed by elements of the 4th Marine Regiment based at the U.S. Marine Corps' Camp Schwab and Camp Hansen. Finally, although not likely, the twenty thousand Marines of the 4th Marine Regiment also offer the option of a rapidly deployable ground force for use either on Taiwan, to secure critical assets in support of Taiwanese ground forces, or even on the Chinese mainland.

Using computer-based combat simulations, a recent study by the RAND Corporation analyzed with some specificity the contribution that Kadena-based F-15 aircraft would likely make in air-to-air engagements with Chinese fighters over Taiwan.[13] The study concluded that the deployment of Kadena-based F-15s alongside Taiwanese fighters would give Taiwan at least a fifty-fifty chance of success against even an extremely robust Chinese force including significant numbers of fourth generation, Russian-designed fighters. Moreover, if the F-15s were paired with the aircraft from a single U.S. carrier battle group, this success rate would increase to eighty percent.[14] This analysis tends to confirm that Kadena-based F-15s could be extremely important, perhaps decisive, in a Taiwan crisis.[15]

Several other potentially China-related military contingencies in the western Pacific could also receive significant support from U.S. forces based in Okinawa. These include a crisis or conflict on the Korean Peninsula, in the South China Sea over Chinese claims to the disputed Spratly Islands, and elsewhere along the eastern or southeastern coastline of China as a result of a growing Sino-American strategic rivalry. Strike aircraft, surveillance and reconnaissance aircraft, command and control aircraft, aerial refueling aircraft, transports, ASW patrol planes, and other air assets based at Kadena Air Base could greatly augment U.S. deterrence and/or warfighting operations in all such situations. Moreover, the twenty thousand Marines of the 4th Marine Regiment and the U.S. Army First Special Forces Group could provide critical assistance to U.S.-led United Nations and South Korean forces in a Korea contingency. However, in none of these instances — with the possible exception of Okinawa-based Marine and Army deployments to Korea[16] — would U.S. forces in Okinawa play as potentially significant a role as in a Taiwan-related contingency.

A Chinese Threat to Okinawa

The very existence of Okinawa-based U.S. forces as both deterrence and warfighting assets in several China-related contingencies automatically links the island to the U.S.-China relationship in a very tangible and potentially dangerous manner. Absent the removal of the above U.S. air and Marine forces from Okinawa, the provision by the United States of a credible and convincing guarantee that such U.S. forces would not be deployed in a China-oriented military contingency, or the conveyance of a credible commitment by Tokyo not to approve the use of U.S. forces in any China-related contingency (all discussed below), Beijing would almost certainly regard Okinawa as a potentially hostile location in a crisis or conflict with the United States. As a result, Okinawa (and therefore the Japanese government) could be exposed to Chinese diplomatic and military coercion before, during, and after such a crisis or conflict, and perhaps in extremis, even to a military attack. This would particularly be the case if a Sino-American confrontation occurred over the Taiwan issue, given the high utility of Okinawa- and Yokohama/Kanto Plain-based U.S. forces in such a contingency.

In fact, it appears that Beijing has already given some thought — and perhaps taken some actions — aimed at influencing both U.S. and Japanese calculations regarding Okinawa in a Taiwan crisis. Although U.S. bases in Okinawa have been within range of Chinese medium- and long-range ballistic missiles for many years,[17] such missiles have been few in number, relatively inaccurate, and probably intended as a strategic deterrent against the possible employment (or threat of employment) of U.S. nuclear weapons the Chinese believe might be based in Okinawa. It now appears, however, that the Chinese military is developing an extended-range version of their short-range CSS-6/M-9 ballistic missile that is capable of striking U.S. forces in Okinawa (and perhaps elsewhere in Japan) with considerable accuracy and in significant numbers.[18] The development and deployment of this relatively inexpensive yet sophisticated, solid-fuelled, mobile missile would result in a significant increase in the number of highly accurate conventional — and perhaps unconventional — warheads that could be directed at Okinawa over the near to medium term.[19] It is far from clear that the Chinese government would actually threaten, much less employ, ballistic missiles (or other weapons such as long-range bombers or even naval assets) against targets in Okinawa and other parts of Japan in a crisis with the United States. Nonetheless, the very existence of such growing Chinese capabilities, combined with the perceived threat to China posed by U.S. forces in Okinawa, present genuine concerns.[20]

Options for Okinawa

Given the obvious danger to Okinawa presented by the development of a potentially robust Chinese missile (or perhaps air or naval) threat, the question arises as to what Okinawa, the Japanese government, the United States, or other powers can or should do to minimize — or if possible eliminate — that threat. Obviously, one option is to press for the complete removal of all relevant U.S. air and ground forces from Okinawa. Such an option, however, is entirely unrealistic.[21] Even if limited only to Okinawa, the withdrawal of most U.S. air and ground forces would be extremely damaging to both Japanese and American interests under current circumstances. U.S. forces in Okinawa could be employed in numerous contingencies of obvious importance to the security of the Japanese nation, such as a conflict on the Korean Peninsula and even the defense of the main Japanese islands. Even more important, any effort to eject major U.S. forces from Okinawa — in particular the air assets at Kadena Air Base — would undoubtedly place a severe strain on the U.S.-Japan Security Alliance. This is especially true given the high value placed on such assets by the U.S. government as a critical element of America's forward-deployed presence in Asia, and the lack of alternative basing locations for such forces in the western Pacific. The redeployment of these forces to locations such as Guam or to bases in central or northern Japan (such as the U.S. Air Force's Misawa Air Base) would be either highly impracticable or would, in the view of defense planners concerned with a Taiwan crisis, probably place them too far from the Taiwan Strait, thus severely reducing their utility.

A second option is to obtain a credible commitment from the United States not to employ Okinawa-based U.S. forces in any China-related crisis or conflict between Beijing and Washington, or in any crisis regarding Taiwan in particular. This is also highly unrealistic and would probably prove ineffective even if possible. Although the U.S. government cannot assume that Tokyo would automatically approve the deployment of its Okinawa-based forces in a China-related military contingency — given the ambiguity of the Japanese position on this issue (discussed below) — it certainly would not want to rule out the use of those forces in advance of a crisis. As indicated above, U.S. air assets in Okinawa could prove critical in a Taiwan conflict. Although the U.S. Pacific Command in Hawai'i has undoubtedly developed operational plans regarding Taiwan (and perhaps other potential China-related contingencies) that do not depend on the use of Okinawa-based assets, such plans would almost certainly pose greater risks and complexities and hence offer a reduced chance of success. This would especially be the case if the U.S. needed to deploy significant air assets to Taiwan in the opening days of a conflict, as discussed above. Given such considerations, any attempt to press vigorously for a U.S. assurance could severely damage the U.S.-Japan Security Alliance. Moreover, it is highly unlikely that China would accept such a U.S. assurance. It is something akin to mutual non-targeting agreements regarding nuclear weapons: although politically useful as a confidence-building measure, it can be easily reversed — as long as the underlying capability remains in place — and thus has little effect on military and strategic calculations.

A third option is to inform the U.S. government (and probably Beijing as well) that Japan would not approve the deployment of any Okinawa-based U.S. forces against China in the event of a Sino-American military-political crisis. Japan is not explicitly obligated by either Article Six of the U.S.-Japan Security Treaty or the revised Guidelines for U.S.-Japan Defense Cooperation to approve the deployment of U.S. forces based in Japan for such uses. On the contrary, Japan's stance regarding such military contingencies outside the main islands remains intentionally vague. For example, the revised Defense Guidelines offer only general references to unspecified levels of bilateral defense cooperation "...in situations in areas surrounding Japan that will have an impact on Japan's peace and security." Moreover, the government of Japan has officially interpreted this phrase as meaning that the implementation of the revised Guidelines would be situational and is not aimed at any particular issue or area.[22]

This suggests that Japan probably retains the authority to deny the use of U.S. forces in Okinawa in the event of a China-related crisis. However, any such decision would also pose the kind of grave potential danger to the U.S.-Japan Security Alliance mentioned above. In fact, the impact on the alliance would likely be even more severe in this instance, since it is difficult to conceive how Tokyo could deny approval for the deployment of U.S. forces in Okinawa and not include in this proscription the American aircraft carrier located at the Yokosuka Naval Base in Yokohama. As suggested above, this Japan-based U.S. carrier would almost certainly be essential to any effective U.S. military response in a Taiwan military crisis of whatever type; denying its use during such a situation would precipitate a major crisis in U.S.-Japan relations.

Of course, Tokyo might eventually deny Washington permission to deploy forces from Japan during a U.S.-China military-political crisis for very understandable reasons rooted in the specific context of the crisis, e.g., if the U.S. were viewed by Japan (and perhaps other countries) as having provoked the crisis, and/or if Japan strongly believed that the deployment of U.S. military forces would exacerbate the situation at hand. Such a potentially momentous decision — still involving considerable political and security risks for Japan — could not be taken prior to the advent of a crisis, and therefore would not reduce the existing threat to Okinawa.

A fourth option is to lower the likelihood of any Chinese threat against Okinawa by reducing the overall utility of Okinawa-based U.S. forces in a Sino-American crisis over Taiwan. Three basic means exist to achieve this objective. One approach would require the United States to reduce the size of those U.S. forces in Okinawa most appropriate to a Taiwan contingency. These forces include, in order of likely importance, air interception and strike aircraft, sustainment and support facilities and aircraft, surveillance and reconnaissance aircraft, ASW aircraft, and ground forces. However, reducing — rather than eliminating — these forces in any meaningful way (i.e., to an extent that such reductions significantly lower Chinese concerns over Okinawa-based U.S. forces) would prove to be extremely difficult. It would be virtually impossible to determine the level of reductions necessary to reduce Chinese concerns without seriously degrading Japanese and U.S. security missions in the main islands and beyond. Many of the same factors cited above would likely come into play (e.g., the creation of strains in the U.S.-Japan Security Alliance). And even if deemed possible, it is highly unlikely that redeployments would occur in sufficient numbers, and in a sufficiently timely manner,[23] to affect China's calculus regarding Okinawa.

A second means would be to increase significantly the ability of U.S. forces outside Okinawa to come to the assistance of Taiwan very quickly and with sufficient force. This would likely require major advances in the readiness level of U.S. air assets in the Pacific and beyond, and/or significant increases in the number and capability of those forces located in the western Pacific. The United States is currently undertaking such improvements in its force posture. However, the improvements attained in force readiness and presence would need to be of a magnitude sufficient to convince the Chinese that the U.S. would have virtually no incentive to deploy Okinawa-based forces, even in the case of the sort of rapid, fait accompli-oriented strike outlined above. This is highly unlikely, unless perhaps the Japanese government were to strenuously resist such a deployment.

The third means would require the United States and Taiwan to greatly augment the latter's ability to deter or defeat a Chinese attack — and especially a rapid Chinese attack — without the assistance of U.S. forces. Washington is currently engaged in an intense, and deepening, effort to assist Taipei in strengthening its military capabilities. Although some clear progress has been achieved thus far, much remains to be done and many serious economic, political, technical, bureaucratic, and even historical obstacles must be overcome before truly major advances are possible. More important, even if Taiwan's military is significantly strengthened as a result of these efforts, it is highly problematic that such improvements would obviate the need for significant U.S. military assistance, especially in the event of a fait accompli-oriented attack.[24]

A fifth option is for Japan to acquire an effective ballistic missile defense (BMD) system, in order to neutralize or greatly minimize the threat to Okinawa (and perhaps to U.S. bases in other parts of Japan) posed by China's expanding medium-range ballistic missile force. In recent months, Tokyo has shown a greater desire to develop and deploy — with significant U.S. assistance — some type of BMD system, largely as a result of the deepening crisis over North Korea's nuclear weapons and ballistic missile programs. Major obstacles to the attainment of this goal exist, however, especially if the purpose of such a BMD system is to protect against the much more sophisticated and larger ballistic missile threat posed by China. In brief, it remains highly uncertain as to whether Japan and the United States have the funds and the technological capability to develop and deploy a BMD system of sufficient size and reliability to protect Okinawa from potentially hundreds of Chinese ballistic missiles, within the five to ten year time period that many analysts believe a crisis over Taiwan might occur.[25] Moreover, the acquisition of even an effective BMD system would not protect Okinawa from other forms of attack, such as air or naval bombardment by cruise missiles or bombs.

A sixth option is for Tokyo — and perhaps Okinawa — to exert its utmost diplomatic effort to reduce the chance that the United States and China will become embroiled in a military-political crisis over Taiwan or other issues in the western Pacific involving China, such as the Spratly Islands dispute. This option is arguably the most realistic and practicable one for Japan, given the clear dangers and complexities presented by the above alternatives. However, even this option is far from risk-free, and might not have enormous utility. As a close ally of the United States, Japan cannot distance itself too much from U.S. policy toward China and Taiwan. Nonetheless, Tokyo could contribute to the stabilization of the U.S.-China relationship by undertaking a variety of actions that would likely be acceptable to Washington. For example, Japanese officials could emphasize repeatedly and officially at the highest levels that Japan does not view China as an emerging strategic threat and that it has no interest in pressing for the permanent separation of Taiwan from mainland China, as some Chinese suspect. To reinforce this stance, senior Japanese officials could also repeatedly stress Japan's continued commitment to the "One China" policy and their desire for both Beijing and Taipei to refrain from undertaking any provocative political or military actions. Tokyo could also exert greater efforts to develop a regular series of strategic dialogues with both China and the United States concerning security issues in Northeast Asia, to deepen understanding and cooperation in managing common concerns such as the Taiwan issue, as well as any other issues emerging from the continued "rise" of China. Japan could also strive to develop specific military and political confidence-building measures with China that reduce the chances of inadvertent crises emerging over potential hotspots. In addition, Japan could press for more and deeper bilateral consultations with the United States regarding policy toward China, to avoid any sudden or surprising shifts in U.S. policy.

Any of these measures might reduce the chances of a Sino-American crisis of the sort that could pose significant security risks for Okinawa. It is unlikely, however, that such actions will entirely eliminate, or perhaps even significantly lessen, the potential dangers that Okinawa faces as a result of the presence of major U.S. forces and the association of those forces with an inherently uncertain Sino-American relationship. To a certain extent, those dangers are unavoidable given the military and political realities discussed above. At the same time, it should be recognized that U.S. forces in Okinawa, as a critical component of U.S. forces in Japan, perform a very positive, stabilizing function in reassuring both Japan and other nations in the Asia-Pacific that the United States remains committed to its unique and vital security role as an "honest broker" in the region.

---

[1] The following analysis of the current state of U.S.-China relations is primarily drawn from Michael D. Swaine, "Reverse Course: The Fragile Turnaround in U.S.-China Relations," *Policy Brief Number 22*, Carnegie Endowment for International Peace, Washington, D.C., February 2003.

2   For further details on China's more confident foreign policy stance, see Michael D. Swaine, "China: Exploiting a Strategic Opening," in Ashley J. Tellis and Michael Wills, eds., *Strategic Asia 2004–05: Confronting Terrorism in the Pursuit of Power*, National Bureau of Asian Research, Seattle, Washington, 2004.

3   Michael D. Swaine and Ashley J. Tellis, *Interpreting China's Grand Strategy: Past, Present, and Future*, RAND Project Air Force, MR-1121-AF, Santa Monica, California, 2000.

4   Swaine and Tellis, *Interpreting China's Grand Strategy: Past, Present, and Future*, and Swaine, "Reverse Course: The Fragile Turnaround in U.S.-China Relations."

5   Chas. W. Freeman, Jr., "Preventing War in the Taiwan Strait: Restraining Taiwan–and Beijing," *Foreign Affairs*, Council on Foreign Relations, Washington, D.C., July/August 1998.

6   For a more detailed examination of the dangerous dynamic that has emerged between Taiwan and China over the past decade or so, see Michael D. Swaine and James C. Mulvenon, *Taiwan's Foreign and Defense Policies: Features and Determinants*, RAND Center for Asia-Pacific Policy, Santa Monica, California, 2001, especially chapters three and four.

7   Effective deterrence of China cannot rest upon Taiwan's military forces alone.   Given the growing capability of China's military forces, the island will probably not acquire the capability to credibly damage or defeat on its own a sustained assault by the mainland.

8   Thomas J. Christensen, "Posing Problems without Catching Up: China's Rise and Challenges for U.S. Security Policy," *International Security* 25:4, Spring 2001.

9   Such an attack is deemed very possible by the Pentagon. See U.S. Department of Defense, "Report to Congress Pursuant to the FY2000 National Defense Authorization Act: Annual Report on the Military Power of the People's Republic of China," 28 July 2003. Unfortunately, it is unclear to this observer whether the Taiwanese air force is currently capable of mounting a rapid and powerful air defense on its own. In any event, the potential ability of the United States to deploy two squadrons of F-15s to the Taiwan Strait in relatively short order arguably constitutes an important deterrent factor.

10 Among these forces, the U.S. aircraft carrier based in Yokohama would be the most important source of U.S. firepower beyond Okinawa. It would almost certainly be dispatched to Taiwan within hours of a military crisis, or possibly in advance of a crisis. Yet it would require several days — perhaps a week — to bring its aircraft to within striking distance of the Taiwan Strait.

11 According to at least one knowledgeable informant, one should also consider the possibility that the most easily available long-range aircraft deployable to Taiwan on short notice would likely consist of B-2 or B-52 bombers, not smaller, shorter-range interceptor or strike aircraft. The availability of bombers over fighters would arguably skew the options available to U.S. decision makers in a crisis toward bombing missions as opposed to air-to-air interception missions, thus increasing the risk of unwanted escalation.

[12] That said, it is probably also the case that Kadena's existing infrastructure cannot at present support a major, rapid increase in the U.S. force presence. The limits on the capacity of Kadena (and other U.S. military facilities in Okinawa) to handle increasing U.S. force levels is unknown to the author.

[13] The study essentially analyzed scenarios in which U.S.-Taiwan and Chinese aircraft fought one other to attain air superiority over the Taiwan Strait, on the assumption that such superiority was essential to the success of most Chinese coercive campaigns against Taiwan.

[14] David A. Shlapak, David T. Orletsky, Barry A. Wilson, *Dire Strait? Military Aspects of the China-Taiwan Confrontation and Options for U.S. Policy*, RAND, MR-1217-SRF, 2000, pp.38-40, 48.

[15] The importance of Kadena-based combat aircraft is further reinforced by the fact that a single carrier would be unable to mount round-the-clock missions over several days. It would require the equivalent of two carriers (i.e., one carrier and Kadena-based aircraft) to perform this duty.

[16] Yet in the case of a Korea contingency, it is far from clear that the deployment of Okinawa-based U.S. forces would exert a sizeable impact (adverse or otherwise) on U.S.-China relations.

[17] Michael D. Swaine with Loren H. Runyon, *Ballistic Missiles and Missile Defense in Asia*, NBR Analysis: Volume 13, No.3, June 2002, National Bureau of Asian Research, Seattle, Washington, 2002.

[18] U.S. Department of Defense, "Report to Congress Pursuant to the FY2000 National Defense Authorization Act: Annual Report on the Military Power of the People's Republic of China," 28 July 2003.

[19] At least one senior U.S. defense official stated that China might be using such missile deployments against Okinawa "to checkmate or deter or threaten U.S. involvement" if conflict erupts in the Taiwan Strait. See "Strategy Menaces Taiwan, Report Says," *International Herald Tribune*, citing an Associated Press story dated 31 July 2003. Also, see "Pentagon Says China Refitting Missiles to Hit Okinawa," *Washington Times*, 31 July 2003.

[20] It is worth pointing out that Chinese military analysts of a possible future Taiwan crisis generally focus far more attention on the threat posed to the PLA by U.S. aircraft carriers than on land-based air and ground assets located in Okinawa. Yet this should not necessarily be taken as an indication that Okinawa is not regarded as a potential threat. Chinese strategists might believe that Okinawa-based U.S. forces could be neutralized relatively quickly in a crisis, via military action or diplomatic and/or military pressure on the Japanese government. Alternatively, they might think that U.S. forces in Okinawa are too few in number to make a decisive difference in a Taiwan conflict. They might even believe that possible Chinese coercive actions against Okinawa are too sensitive to discuss on anything other than a highly classified basis, given the fact that Beijing and Tokyo have a Treaty of Peace and Friendship.

[21] Although a reduction in the size of the Marine presence on the island might be feasible and desirable for a variety of reasons, that action alone would have little effect on the concerns discussed above. As suggested, the U.S. air

assets in Okinawa would be of far greater importance in a crisis or conflict with China.

22 David J. Richardson, "U.S.-Japan Defense Cooperation: Possibilities for Regional Stability," *Parameters*, Summer 2000, pp.94-104.

23 Some analysts believe that a major political-military crisis over Taiwan could occur as early as 2007–08, for a variety of reasons. It is unlikely that U.S. forces could be moved out of Okinawa in sufficient numbers by that time, even if a willingness to do so existed.

24 For a detailed examination of Taiwan's military modernization and defense reform effort, see Michael D. Swaine, "Taiwan's Defense Reforms and Military Modernization Program: Objectives, Achievements, and Obstacles," in Nancy B. Tucker, ed., *No Way Out? New Thoughts on the U.S.-Taiwan-China Crisis* (forthcoming).

25 See Michael D. Swaine with Loren H. Runyon, *Ballistic Missiles and Missile Defense in Asia*.

Location of U.S. Military Bases in Okinawa

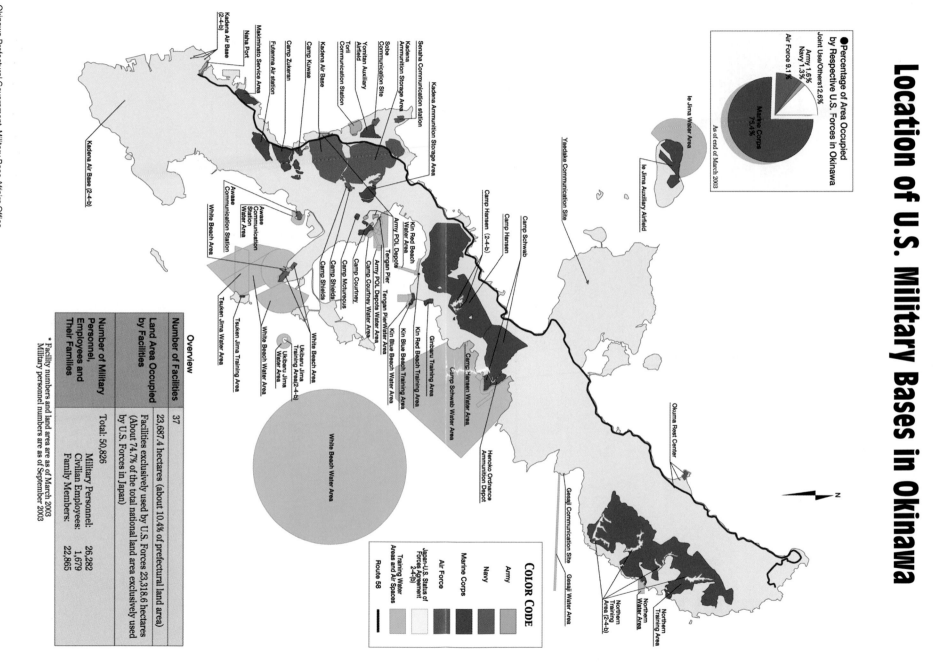

Airports of Okinawa

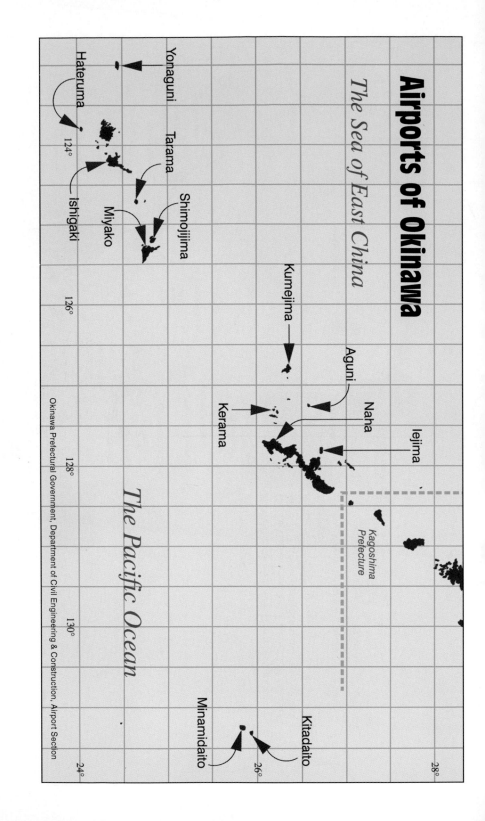

Okinawa Prefectural Government, Department of Civil Engineering & Construction, Airport Section

Air Spaces and Water Areas Used for U.S. Forces Training in Okinawa

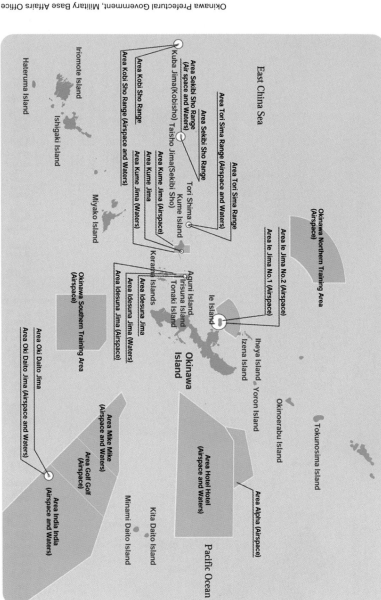

Okinawa Prefectural Government, Military Base Affairs Office

Appendix 1

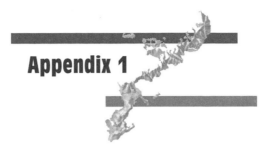

Japan Defense Agency
The SACO Final Report

December 2, 1996
by
Minister for Foreign Affairs Ikeda
Minister of State for Defense Kyuma
Secretary of Defense Perry
Ambassador Mondale

The Special Action Committee on Okinawa (SACO) was established in November 1995 by the Governments of Japan and the United States. The two Governments launched the SACO process to reduce the burden on the people of Okinawa and thereby strengthen the Japan-US alliance.

The mandate and guidelines for the SACO process were set forth by the Governments of Japan and the United States at the outset of the joint endeavor. Both sides decided that the SACO would develop recommendations for the Security Consultative Committee (SCC) on ways to realign, consolidate and reduce US facilities and areas, and adjust operational procedures of US forces in Okinawa consistent with their respective obligations under the Treaty of Mutual Cooperation and Security and other related agreements. The work of the SACO was scheduled to conclude after one year.

The SCC which was held on April 15, 1996, approved the SACO Interim Report which included several significant initiatives, and instructed the SACO to complete and recommend plans with concrete implementation schedules by November 1996.

The SACO, together with the Joint Committee, has conducted a series of intensive and detailed discussions and developed concrete plans and measures to implement the recommendations set forth in the Interim Report.

Today, at the SCC, Minister Ikeda, Minister Kyuma, Secretary Perry and Ambassador Mondale approved this SACO Final Report. The plans and measures included in this Final Report, when implemented, will reduce the impact of the activities of US forces on communities in Okinawa. At the same time, these measures will fully maintain the capabilities and readiness of US forces in Japan while addressing security and force protection requirements. Approximately 21 percent of the total acreage of the US facilities and areas in Okinawa excluding joint use facilities and areas (approx. 5,002 ha/12,361 acres) will be returned.

Upon approving the Final Report, the members of the SCC welcomed the successful conclusion of the year-long SACO process and underscored their strong resolve to continue joint efforts to ensure steady and prompt implementation of the plans and measures of the SACO Final Report. With this understanding, the SCC designated the Joint Committee as the primary forum for bilateral coordination in the implementation phase, where specific conditions for the completion of each item will be addressed. Coordination with local communities will take place as necessary.

The SCC also reaffirmed the commitment of the two governments to make every endeavor to deal with various issues related to the presence and status of US forces, and to enhance mutual understanding between US forces and local Japanese communities. In this respect, the SCC agreed that efforts to these ends should continue, primarily through coordination at the Joint Committee.

The members of the SCC agreed that the SCC itself and the Security Sub-Committee (SSC) would monitor such coordination at the Joint Committee described above and provide guidance as appropriate. The SCC also instructed the SSC to seriously address the Okinawa-related issues as one of the most important subjects and regularly report back to the SCC on this subject.

In accordance with the April 1 996 Japan-US Joint Declaration on Security, the SCC emphasized the importance of close consultation on the international situation, defense policies and military postures, bilateral policy coordination and efforts towards a more peaceful and stable security environment in the Asia- Pacific region. The SCC instructed the SSC to pursue these goals and to address the Okinawa-related issues at the same time.

Return Land

■ **Futenma Air Station** (see Appendix 2)

■ **Northern Training Area**

Return major portion of the Northern Training Area (approx. 3,987 ha/9,852 acres) and release US joint use of certain reservoirs (approx. 159 ha/393 acres) with the intention to finish the process by the end of March 2003 under the following conditions:

Provide land area (approx. 38 ha/93 acres) and water area (approx. 121 ha/298 acres) with the intention to finish the process by the end of March 1998 in order to ensure access from the remaining Northern Training Area to the ocean. Relocate helicopter landing zones from the areas to be returned to the remaining Northern Training Area.

■ **Aha Training Area**

Release US joint use of Aha Training Area (approx. 480 ha/1,185 acres) and release US joint use of the water area (approx. 7,895 ha/19,509 acres) with the intention to finish the process by the end of March 1998 after land and water access areas from the Northern Training Area to the ocean are provided.

■ **Gimbaru Training Area**

Return Gimbaru Training Area (approx. 60 ha/149 acres) with the intention to finish the process by the end of March 1 998 after the helicopter landing zone is relocated to Kin Blue Beach Training Area, and the other facilities are relocated to Camp Hansen.

■ **Sobe Communication Site**

Return Sobe Communication Site (approx. 53 ha/132 acres) with the intention to finish the process by the end of March 2001 after the antenna facilities and associated support facilities are relocated to Camp Hansen.

■ **Yomitan Auxiliary Airfield**

Return Yomitan Auxiliary Airfield (approx. 191 ha/471 acres) with the intention to finish the process by the end of March 2001 after the parachute drop training is relocated to Ie Jima Auxiliary Airfield and Sobe Communication Site is relocated.

■ **Camp Kuwae**

Return most of Camp Kuwae (approx. 99 ha/245 acres) with the intention to finish the process by the end of March 2008 after the Naval Hospital is relocated to Camp Zukeran and remaining facilities there are relocated to Camp Zukeran or other US facilities and areas in Okinawa.

■ **Senaha Communication Station**

Return Senaha Communication Station (approx. 61 ha/151 acres) with the intention to finish the process by the end of March 2001 after the antenna facilities and associated support facilities are relocated to Torii Communication Station. However, the microwave tower portion (approx. 0.1 ha/0.3 acres) will be retained.

■ **Makiminato Service Area**

Return land adjacent to Route 58 (approx. 3 ha/8 acres) in order to widen the Route, after the facilities which will be affected by the return are relocated withinthe remaining Makiminato Service Area.

■ **Naha Port**

Jointly continue best efforts to accelerate the return of Naha Port (approx. 57 ha/140 acres) in connection to its relocation to the Urasoe Pier area (approx. 35 ha/87 acres).

■ **Housing consolidation (Camp Kuwae and Camp Zukeran)**

Consolidate US housing areas in Camp Kuwae and Camp Zukeran and return portions of land in housing areas there with the intention to finish the process by the end of March 2008 (approx. 83 ha/206 acres at Camp Zukeran; in addition, approx. 35 ha/85 acres at Camp Kuwae will be returned through housing consolidation. That land amount is included in the above entry on Camp Kuwae.).

Adjust Training and Operational Procedures

■ **Artillery live-fire training over Highway 104**

Terminate artillery live-fire training over Highway 104, with the exception of artillery firing required in the event of a crisis, after the training is relocated to maneuver areas on the mainland of Japan within Japanese Fiscal Year 1997.

■ **Parachute drop training**

Relocate parachute drop training to Ie Jima Auxiliary Airfield.

■ **Conditioning hikes on public roads**

Conditioning hikes on public roads have been terminated.

Implement Noise Reduction Initiatives

■ **Aircraft noise abatement countermeasures at Kadena Air Base and Futenma Air Station**

Agreements on aircraft noise abatement countermeasures at Kadena Air Base and Futenma Air Station announced by the Joint Committee in March 1996 have been implemented.

■ **Transfer of KC-130 Hercules aircraft and AV-8 Harrier aircraft**

Transfer 12 KC-130 aircraft currently based at Futenma Air Station to Iwakuni Air Base after adequate facilities are provided. Transfer of 14 AV-8 aircraft from Iwakuni Air Base to the United States has been completed.

■ **Relocation of Navy aircraft and MC-130 operations at Kadena Air Base**

Relocate Navy aircraft operations and supporting facilities at Kadena Air Base from the Navy ramp to the other side of the major runways. The implementation schedules for these measures will be decided along with the implementation schedules for the development of additional facilities at Kadena Air Base necessary for the return of Futenma Air Station. Move the MC-130s at Kadena Air Base from the Navy ramp to the northwest corner of the major runways by the end of December 1996.

- **Noise reduction baffles at Kadena Air Base**

Build new noise reduction baffles at the north side of Kadena Air Base with the intention to finish the process by the end of March 1998.

- **Limitation of night flight training operations at Futenma Air Station**

Limit night flight training operations at Futenma Air Station to the maximum extent possible, consistent with the operational readiness of US forces.

Improve Status of Forces Agreement Procedures:

- **Accident reports**

Implement new Joint Committee agreement on procedures to provide investigation reports on US military aircraft accidents announced on December 2, 1996.

In addition, as part of the US forces' good neighbor policy, every effort will be made to insure timely notification of appropriate local officials, as well as the Government of Japan, of all major accidents involving US forces' assets or facilities.

- **Public exposure of Joint Committee agreements**

Seek greater public exposure of Joint Committee agreements.

- **Visits to US facilities and areas**

Implement the new procedures for authorizing visits to US facilities and areas announced by the Joint Committee on December 2, 1996.

- **Markings on US forces official vehicles**

Implement the agreement on measures concerning markings on US forces official vehicles. Numbered plates will be attached to all non-tactical US forces vehicles by January 1997, and to all other US forces vehicles by October 1997.

- **Supplemental automobile insurance**

Education programs for automobile insurance have been expanded. Additionally, on its own initiative, the US has further elected to have all personnel under the SOFA obtain supplemental auto insurance beginning in January 1997.

- **Payment for claims**

Make joint efforts to improve payment procedures concerning claims under paragraph 6, Article XVIII of the SOFA in the following manner:

Requests for advance payments will be expeditiously processed and evaluated by both Governments utilizing their respective procedures. Whenever warranted under US laws and regulatory guidance, advance payment will be accomplished as rapidly as possible.

A new system will be introduced by the end of March 1998, by which Japanese authorities will make available to claimants no-interest loans, as appropriate, in advance of the final adjudication of claims by US authorities.

In the past there have been only a very few cases where payment by the US Government did not satisfy the full amount awarded by a final court judgment. Should such a case occur in the future, the Government of Japan will endeavor to make payment to the claimant, as appropriate, in order to address the difference in amount.

■ **Quarantine procedures**

Implement the updated agreement on quarantine procedures announced by the Joint Committee on December 2, 1996.

■ **Removal of unexploded ordnance in Camp Hansen**

Continue to use USMC procedures for removing unexploded ordnance in Camp Hansen, which are equivalent to those applied to ranges of the US forces in the United States.

■ **Continue efforts to improve the SOFA procedures in the Joint Committee**

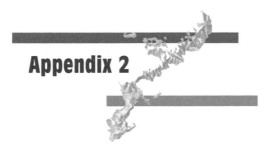

Appendix 2

Japan Defense Agency
The SACO Final Report on Futenma
(an integral part of the SACO Final Report)

Tokyo, Japan
December 2, 1996

Introduction

At the Security Consultative Committee (SCC) held on December 2, 1996, Mister Ikeda, Mister Kyuma, Secretary Perry, and Ambassador Mondale reaffirmed their commitment to the Special Action Committee on Okinawa (SACO) Interim Report of April 15, 1996 and the Status Report of September 19, 1996. Based on the SACO Interim Report, both Governments have been working to determine a suitable option for the return of Futenma Air Station and the relocation of its assets to other facilities and areas in Okinawa, while maintaining the airfield's critical military functions and capabilities. The Status Report called for the Special working Group on Futenma to examine three specific alternatives: 1) incorporate the heliport into Kadena Air Base; 2) construct a heliport at Camp Schwab ; and 3) develop and construct a sea-based facility (SBF).

On December 2, 1996, the SCC approved the SACO recommendation to pursue the SBF option. Compared to the other two options, the SBF is judged to be the best option in tens of enhanced safety and quality-of-life for the Okinawan people while maintaining operational capabilities of U.S. forces. In addition, the SBF can function as a fixed facility during its use as a military base and can also be removed when no longer necessary.

The SCC will establish a bilateral U.S.-Japan working group under the supervision of the Security Sub-Committee (SSC) entitled the Futenma Implementation Group (FIG), to be supported by a team of technical experts. The FIG, working with the Joint Committee, will develop a plan for implementation no later than December 1997. Upon SCC approval of this plan, the FIG, working with the Joint Committee, will oversee design, construction, testing, and transfer of assets.

Decisions of the SCC

■ Pursue construction of the SBF to absorb most of the helicopter operational functions of Futenma Air Station. This facility will be approximately 1500 meters long, and will support the majority of Futenma Air Station's flying operations, including an Instrument Flight Rules (IFR)-capable runway (approximately 1300 meters long), direct air operations support, and indirect support infrastructure such as headquarters, maintenance, logistics, quality-oflife functions, and base operating support. The SBF will be designed to support basing of helicopter assets, and will also be able to support short-field aircraft operations.

■ Transfer 12 KC-130 aircraft to Iwakuni Air Base. Construct facilities at this base to ensure that associated infrastructure is available to support these aircraft and their missions.

■ Develop additional facilities at Kadena Air Base to support aircraft, maintenance, and logistics operations which are currently available at Futenma Air Station but are not relocated to the SBF or Iwakuni Air Base.

■ Study the emergency and contingency use of alternate facilities which may be needed in the event of a crisis. This is necessary because the transfer of functions from Futenma Air Station to the SBF will reduce operational flexibility currently available.

■ Return Futenma Air Station within the next five to seven years, after adequate replacement facilities are completed and operational.

Guiding Principles

■ Futenma Air Station's critical military functions and capabilities will be maintained and will continue to operate at current readiness levels throughout the transfer of personnel and equipment and the relocation of facilities.

■ To the greatest extent possible, Futenma Air Station's operations and activities will be transferred to the SBF. Operational capabilities and contingency planning flexibility which cannot be supported by the shorter runway of the SBF (such as strategic airlift logistics, emergency alternate divert, and contingency throughput) must be fully supported elsewhere. Those facilities unable to be located on the SBF, due to operational, cost, or quality-of-life considerations, will be located on existing US facilities and areas.

■ The SBF will be located off the east coast of the main island of Okinawa, and is expected to be connected to land by a pier or causeway. Selection of the location will take into account operational requirements, air-space and sea-lane deconfliction, fishing access, environmental compatibility, economic effects, noise abatement, survivability, security, and convenient, acceptable personnel access to other US military facilities and housing.

- The design of the SBF will incorporate adequate measures to ensure platform, aircraft, equipment, and personnel survivability against severe weather and ocean conditions; corrosion control treatment and prevention for the SBF and all equipment located on the SBF; safety and platform security Support will include reliable and secure fuel supply, electrical power, fresh water, and other utilities and consumables. Additionally, the facility will be fully self-supporting for short-period contingency/emergency operations.
- The Government of Japan will provide the SBF and other relocation facilities for the use of U.S. forces, in accordance with the U.S.-Japan Treaty of Mutual Cooperation and Security and the Status of Forces Agreement. The two Governments will further consider all aspects of life-cycle costs as part of the design/acquisition decision.
- The Government of Japan will continue to keep the people of Okinawa informed of the progress of this plan, including concept, location, and schedules of implementation.

Possible Sea-Based Facility Construction Methods

Studies have been conducted by a "Technical Support Group" comprised of Government engineers under the guidance of a "Technical Advisory Group" comprised of university professors and other experts outside the Government. These studies suggested that all three construction methods mentioned below are technically feasible.

- Pile Supported Pier Type (using floating modules) — supported by a number of steel columns fixed to the sea bed.
- Pontoon Type — platform consisting of steel pontoon type units, installed in a calm sea protected by a breakwater.
- Semi-Submersible Type — platform at a wave free height, supported by buoyancy of the lower structure submerged under the sea.

The Next Steps

- The FIG will recommend a candidate SBF area to ale SCC as soon as possible and formulate a detailed implementation plan no later than December 1997. This plan win include completion of ale following items: concept development and definition of operational requirements, technology performance specifications and construction method, site survey, environmental analysis, and final concept and site selection.
- The FIG will establish phases and schedules to achieve operational capabilities at each location, including facility design, construction, installation of required components, validation tests and suitability demonstrations, and transfer of operations to the new facility.
- The FIG will conduct periodic reviews and make decisions at significant milestones concerning SBF program feasibility.

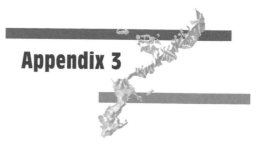

Appendix 3

JOINT STATEMENT
U.S.-JAPAN SECURITY CONSULTATIVE COMMITTEE

Washington, DC
February 19, 2005

United States Secretary of State Condoleezza Rice and Secretary of Defense Donald Rumsfeld hosted Japan's Minister for Foreign Affairs Nobutaka Machimura and Minister of State for Defense and Director-General of the Defense Agency Yoshinori Ohno in a meeting of the Security Consultative Committee (SCC) in Washington, DC, on February 19, 2005. They addressed security and alliance issues facing the United States and Japan, as well as other aspects of the relationship.

Working Together on Challenges Facing the World Today

The Ministers noted the excellent state of cooperative relations between the United States and Japan on a broad array of security, political, and economic issues. They looked to expand that cooperation, recognizing that the U.S.-Japan Alliance, with the U.S.-Japan security arrangements at its core, continues to play a vital role in ensuring the security and prosperity of both the United States and Japan, as well as in enhancing regional and global peace and stability.

The Ministers underscored the importance of U.S. and Japanese leadership in providing international assistance to Afghanistan, Iraq, and the broader Middle East — efforts that are already producing results. The Ministers lauded the successful cooperation between the United States and Japan with other countries in extending wide-ranging assistance to those who suffered from the earthquake and the subsequent tsunami disaster in the Indian Ocean.

The Ministers recognized that cooperation and consultation between the United States and Japan have been pivotal in promoting nonproliferation, particularly through the Proliferation Security

Initiative. They welcomed the success of multinational interdiction exercises hosted by the United States and Japan and by others.

The Ministers expressed their confidence that ballistic missile defense (BMD) enhances our ability to defend against and deter ballistic missile attacks and dissuade other parties from investing in ballistic missiles. Taking note of achievements in missile defense cooperation, such as Japan's decision to introduce ballistic missile defense systems and its recent announcement on its Three Principles on Arms Export, the Ministers reaffirmed their commitment to close cooperation on policy and operational matters and to advancing U.S.-Japan cooperative research in BMD systems, with a view to possible cooperative development.

Common Strategic Objectives

The Ministers discussed the new security environment in which new and emerging threats, such as international terrorism and proliferation of weapons of mass destruction (WMD) and their means of delivery, have surfaced as common challenges. They recognized that deepening interdependence among nations in a global community means that such threats can affect the security of nations worldwide, including the United States and Japan.

While noting that these threats are also emerging in the Asia-Pacific region, the Ministers also emphasized that persistent challenges continue to create unpredictability and uncertainty. Moreover, they noted that modernization of military capabilities in the region also requires attention.

The Ministers strongly urged North Korea to return to the Six-Party Talks expeditiously and without preconditions, and to commit itself to complete dismantlement of all its nuclear programs in a transparent manner subject to verification.

Based on this understanding of the international security environment, the Ministers concurred that both Governments need to work closely together to pursue common strategic objectives through their respective efforts, implementation of the U.S.-Japan security arrangements, and other joint efforts based on the alliance. Both sides decided to hold regular consultations to coordinate policies in accordance with these common strategic objectives and to update these objectives as the security environment requires.

In the region, common strategic objectives include:

- Ensure the security of Japan, strengthen peace and stability in the Asia-Pacific region, and maintain the capability to address contingencies affecting the United States and Japan.

■ Support peaceful unification of the Korean Peninsula.

■ Seek peaceful resolution of issues related to North Korea, including its nuclear programs, ballistic missile activities, illicit activities, and humanitarian issues such as the abduction of Japanese nationals by North Korea.

■ Develop a cooperative relationship with China, welcoming the country to play a responsible and constructive role regionally as well as globally.

■ Encourage the peaceful resolution of issues concerning the Taiwan Strait through dialogue.

■ Encourage China to improve transparency of its military affairs.

■ Encourage Russia's constructive engagement in the Asia-Pacific region.

■ Fully normalize Japan-Russia relations through the resolution of the Northern Territories issue.

■ Promote a peaceful, stable, and vibrant Southeast Asia.

■ Welcome the development of various forms of regional cooperation, while stressing the importance of open, inclusive, and transparent regional mechanisms.

■ Discourage destabilizing sales and transfers of arms and military technology.

■ Maintain the security of maritime traffic.

Global common strategic objectives include:

■ Promote fundamental values such as basic human rights, democracy, and the rule of law in the international community.

■ Further consolidate U.S.-Japan partnership in international peace cooperation activities and development assistance to promote peace, stability, and prosperity worldwide.

■ Promote the reduction and nonproliferation of weapons of mass destruction (WMD) and their means of delivery, including through improved reliability and effectiveness of the Non-Proliferation Treaty, the International Atomic Energy Agency, and other regimes, and initiatives such as the Proliferation Security Initiative.

■ Prevent and eradicate terrorism.

■ Coordinate efforts to improve the effectiveness of the United Nations Security Council by making the best use of the current momentum to realize Japan's aspiration to become a permanent member.

■ Maintain and enhance the stability of the global energy supply.

Strengthening of U.S.-Japan Security and Defense Cooperation

The Ministers expressed their support and appreciation for each other's efforts to develop their respective security and defense policies. Japan's new National Defense Program Guidelines (NDPG) emphasize Japan's capability to respond effectively to new threats and diverse contingencies, Japan's active engagement to improve the international security environment, and the importance of the Japan-U.S. Alliance. As a central component of its broad defense transformation effort, the United States is reorienting and strengthening its global defense posture to provide it with appropriate, strategy-driven capabilities in an uncertain security environment. The Ministers confirmed that these efforts will ensure and strengthen effective security and defense cooperation as both countries pursue common strategic objectives.

In this context, the Ministers underscored the need to continue examining the roles, missions, and capabilities of Japan's Self Defense Forces and the U.S. Armed Forces required to respond effectively to diverse challenges in a well-coordinated manner. This examination will take into account recent achievements and developments such as Japan's NDPG and new legislation to deal with contingencies, as well as the expanded agreement on mutual logistical support and progress in BMD cooperation. The Ministers also emphasized the importance of enhancing interoperability between U.S. and Japanese forces.

The Ministers concurred that this examination should contribute to these consultations on realignment of U.S. force structure in Japan. They decided to intensify these consultations in a comprehensive effort to strengthen the alliance as the bedrock of Japan's security and the anchor of regional stability. In this context, both sides confirmed their commitment to maintaining deterrence and capabilities of U.S. forces in Japan while reducing the burden on local communities, including those in Okinawa. The Ministers directed their staffs to report expeditiously on the results of these consultations.

The Ministers also stressed the importance of continued efforts to enhance positive relations between local communities and U.S. forces. They emphasized that improved implementation of the Status of Forces Agreement (SOFA), including due attention to the environment, and steady implementation of the Special Action Committee on Okinawa (SACO) Final Report are important to the stable presence of U.S. forces in Japan.

The Ministers, noting that the current Special Measures Agreement (SMA) will expire in March 2006, decided to start consultations on future arrangements to provide appropriate levels of host nation support, bearing in mind the significant role of the SMA in supporting the presence of U.S. forces in Japan.

PROFILES OF THE CONTRIBUTORS

Akikazu HASHIMOTO is professor at the National Graduate Institute for Policy Studies in Tokyo, Japan. He previously managed a private think tank, taught at Teikyo University, and was a visiting scholar at the University of Southern California. A specialist of the quantitative analysis of politics, he has written numerous books on public opinion, political attitudes, and electoral behavior. He received his Ph.D. in law from Keio University.

Ryutaro HASHIMOTO was first elected to parliament from Okayama Prefecture in 1963 as a member of the Liberal Democratic Party (LDP). He has served as minister of health and welfare (1978-79), transport (1986-87), finance (1989-91), and international trade and industry (1994-96). He became LDP president in 1995 and served as prime minister from 1996 to 1998. He is author of the book, *Vision of Japan*, and a graduate of Keio University.

Hisayoshi INA is a columnist and member of the editorial board of the Nihon Keizai Shimbun and recipient of the 1998 Vaughn-Uyeda Memorial Prize (Japanese version of the Pulitzer Prize). He is the author of *A Multilateral Approach for the Pacific* and coauthor of *Redefining the Partnership: the United States and Japan in East Asia*. He received his B.A. in political science from Waseda University.

Yoichi KATO is deputy editor of the foreign news department of the Asahi Shimbun. He was previously Asahi's Washington political correspondent and visiting research fellow at both the Institute for National Strategic Studies/National Defense University and the Center for Strategic and International Studies. He received his M.A. in international relations from Tufts University.

Mike M. MOCHIZUKI is director of the Sigur Center for Asian Studies and holder of the Japan-U.S. Relations Chair in Memory of Gaston Sigur at the George Washington University. He was previously a senior fellow at the Brookings Institution, co-director of the Center for Asia-Pacific Policy at RAND, associate professor at the University of Southern California in Los Angeles, and assistant professor at Yale University. He received his Ph.D. in political science from Harvard University.

Koji MURATA is associate professor of diplomatic history in the Department of Political Science at Doshisha University in Kyoto. A specialist of U.S. foreign policy, the history of U.S.-Japan security relations, and Japan's defense policy, he has published two books: *President Carter's U.S. Troop Withdrawal Policy from South Korea* and *First Defense Secretary Forrestal*. He received his Ph.D. in political science from Kobe University.

Kazuhisa OGAWA is a leading military analyst in Japan, currently chairs Japan's Crisis Management Study Unit in the Cabinet Secretariat, and serves as advisor for the Minister of State for Crisis Management. His recent works include *Anti-Terrorism Troops in America, Can Japan Protect Its Borders?, Battling with Risks: How to Face Terrorism, Disasters and Wars,* and *War on Terrorism.* He graduated from the Japan Ground Self-Defense Force Youth Cadet Training Unit.

Michael O'HANLON is a senior fellow in Foreign Policy Studies at the Brookings Institution and adjunct professor at Columbia University. He is the author or co-author of *Crisis on the Korean Peninsula, Protecting the American Homeland, Defense Policy Choices for the Bush Administration, Defending America: The Case for National Missile Defense,* and *Technological Change and the Future of Warfare.* He received his Ph.D. in public and international affairs from Princeton University.

Tsuneo OSHIRO is director of the Center for Asia-Pacific Island Studies and professor of economics in the Faculty of Law and Letters at the University of the Ryukyus. He was a visiting scholar at the Tokyo Institute of Technology and Cambridge University, president of the Okinawa Economic Association, trustee of the Japan Policy Association, and chairman of the Okinawa Administrative Restructuring Committee and the Healthy Sunrise City Planning Committee of Gushikawa City. He received his M.A. in economics from the University of Connecticut.

Sheila A. SMITH is a fellow at the East-West Center in Honolulu, Hawaii. She was previously assistant professor at Boston University and is also affiliated with the Reischauer Institute of Japanese Studies at Harvard University and the Social Science Research Council Global Security and Cooperation Program. She received her Ph.D. in political science from Columbia University.

Michael D. SWAINE is senior associate and co-director of the China Program at the Carnegie Endowment for International Peace. He was previously a senior political scientist in international studies and research director of the Center for Asia-Pacific Policy at RAND. He is author of "The North Korea Nuclear Crisis: A Strategy for Negotiation," "Reverse Course? The Fragile Turnaround in U.S.-China Relations?", and *Ballistic Missiles and Missile Defense in Asia.* He received his Ph.D. from Harvard University.

Kurayoshi TAKARA is professor of history in the Faculty of Law and Letters of the University of the Ryukyus. He was previously a member of the advisory board to Okinawa Governor Keiichi Inamine and member of the first sectional committee of Prime Minister Keizo Obuchi's Commission on Japan's Goals in the 21st Century. He received a master's degree in letters from Kyushu University.

ACKNOWLEDGEMENTS

This project could not have been undertaken without the help of many individuals and organizations. We would like to express our deepest gratitude to all of them.

Hirokazu Nakaima, chairman of the Nansei Shoto Industrial Advancement Center (NIAC), was critical in backing this endeavor from its inception and for raising the funds to undertake it. Mr. Nakaima also provided invaluable advice at every step.

Katsuaki Chinen and Dennis Nakasone served as executive director and liaison officer respectively of the Okinawa Question 2004 Japan-U.S. Action Committee, and Harukazu Nishio and Naoko Namiki of the Do Research Institute contributed as the Japanese secretariat for this project. They all administered the Japanese side of the project with admirable dedication and energy.

The staff of the Sigur Center for Asian Studies did a wonderful job of managing the project on the American side. We would especially like to acknowledge the help of Ikuko Turner, the center's office and financial manager, and the many students of George Washington University's Elliott School of International Affairs who assisted in the March 2004 Washington conference.

We would also like to acknowledge Yuji Uesugi, executive director of the Okinawa Peace Assistance Center (OPAC), and Kyoko Nakamura, OPAC researcher, for their assistance in both the October 2003 Tokyo workshop and the March 2004 Washington conference. We are grateful to Ambassador Yukio Satoh, chairman of the Japan Institute of International Affairs (JIIA), for agreeing to have JIIA host the October 2003 workshop, and to former Prime Minister Ryutaro Hashimoto and former Japanese Diet Member Eisei Ito for attending this workshop and providing their inspiring comments.

Last, but certainly not least, our heartfelt thanks go to those who played a key role in preparing this report for publication. Hideki Rose, program coordinator of the Sigur Center, was magnificent in coordinating the entire manuscript preparation process, correcting the translations of the papers originally drafted in Japanese, and copyediting all of the chapters. He was ably assisted by Luke Johnson, Dennis Nakasone, and Naoko Namiki. We would like to express our appreciation to the Military Base Affairs Office and the Public Relations Division of the Okinawa Prefectural Government and the Okinawa Times for letting us reproduce their maps and photographs in this report. We also thank the designers, Rich and Marcie Pottern, for producing this report efficiently and attractively.

— *Akikazu Hashimoto, Mike Mochizuki, Kurayoshi Takara*